VERN YIP'S
VACATION AT HOME

VERN YIP'S
VACATION AT HOME

DESIGN IDEAS FOR CREATING YOUR
EVERYDAY GETAWAY

VERN YIP

Running Press
PHILADELPHIA

For my mom, Vera, whose boundless love lit the path to my happy life. Fourteen years after her passing, she is still showing me the way every day.

For my sister and brother-in-law, Katherine and Bob, whose unwavering love and support, halfway around the world, always feels next door.

For our children, Gavin and Vera, whose effusive love, enthusiasm for family, and natural propensity for kindness make me swell with pride.

And for my husband, Craig, who's a constant supply of the full force, all-encompassing love that fuels my dreams. You make it all possible.

Running Press
Hachette Book Group
1290 Avenue of the Americas, New York, NY 10104
www.runningpress.com
@Running_Press

Printed in China

Published by Running Press, an imprint of Perseus Books, LLC,
a subsidiary of Hachette Book Group, Inc.
The Running Press name and logo is a trademark of the Hachette Book Group.

The publisher is not responsible for websites (or their content)
that are not owned by the publisher.

Print book cover and interior design by Joshua McDonnell

Library of Congress Control Number: 2019933541

ISBNs: 978-07624-6482-1 (hardcover), 978-07624-6483-8 (ebook)

LREX

10   9   8   7   6   5   4   3   2   1

CONTENTS

INTRODUCTION

What Makes a Home Restful and Relaxing?

Have nothing in your house that you do not know to be useful or beautiful.

—William Morris

My home is my favorite place on the planet and my ultimate retreat. I'd rather be there than anywhere else, including an exotic location or a luxury resort or five-star hotel. That doesn't mean that I don't love visiting new places and staying at beautiful properties. I still get incredibly excited about visiting somewhere for the first time and discovering something new! I always find myself arriving at the same conclusion: my home is equally as relaxing and enjoyable, but with the major advantage of being specifically tailored to my family and me. The things that we love are there. Everything, from furniture to artwork to storage, has been arranged to help us function as smoothly and enjoyably as possible. All our items also hold special memories and have real meaning to us.

In fact, each time I walk through my front door, I am immediately more relaxed, rejuvenated, and reenergized because my home has been purposefully designed to receive me warmly. It wasn't always that way. It took time to tailor it, both functionally and aesthetically. It required thought to address design changes to the "bones" of our home that were making it more stressful than necessary: a backyard dominated by high-maintenance landscaping; a small and isolated kitchen with insufficient storage; a front entrance that ungraciously dumped you into a cramped hallway; recessed can lights sporting incandescent bulbs that seemingly burned out every other week; and no clear storage system for the necessary "stuff" that comes with having two babies only fourteen months apart. All of it contributed to an ever-growing to-do list and a disorganized, challenging, and unpleasant environment. Quite frankly, I was starting to despise spending our precious family time in this house. After figuring out what to do, instituting changes was both relatively easy and quick, and I can say with confidence that our home is now a stress-free place that supports and nurtures the entire family. It's effectively become a vacation home that we happen to live in every day.

So how did I figure out what changes to make to create an everyday home that would relax and rejuvenate us the way being at a top vacation property does? Aside from ensuring that our home contained only the items that we needed and loved, I logged a lot of travel hours, spent a lot of nights away from home, and took plenty of notes on all the things that worked in the properties I visited, as well as many of the things that *didn't* work. In fact, I've been on the road for nearly three decades (mostly for work, but occasionally for pleasure) and have had the opportunity to stay at many of the best properties in the world—and some not-so-great ones—all with lessons to learn. Travel is an essential part of my life and one of the key ways that I stay inspired.

You should not have to spend a lot of
money to "get away from it all" and relax—
you should be able to do that right at home.

As an interior designer, I'm particularly sensitive to design choices, so I started noticing the smart, intentional design decisions that commonly linked the best properties—choices that made them instantly calming and enjoyable; necessary choices that also made them easier to maintain and durable enough to withstand heavy traffic. Although my house has to stand up to two active kids and four large dogs, most hotels and luxury properties have to look great while hundreds (and sometimes thousands) of guests pass through each year.

In this book, we'll talk about the ways "resort thinking" can help us achieve a beautiful, functional home that will rival your favorite getaway. What is so wonderful about strategizing design to make your home as relaxing, as the most incredible resort you can imagine, is that it does not require you to have even stayed in such a place. I've done the work for you! In fact, you should not have to spend a lot of money to "get away from it all" and relax—you should be able to do that right at home, and that is my mission here. That doesn't mean that I find travel to be any less valuable. In fact, I have major wanderlust! As an architectural and interior designer, I gain tremendous insight by

being immersed in a different culture and gaining access to its people, customs, architecture, art, craft, food, and music. In fact, seeing how different cultures all over the world uniquely address many of the same issues that we face here at home always inspires me on new ways to create the most restorative home environment possible. Traveling almost certainly gives me new clues on how to incorporate that vacation-like feeling once I'm back home.

No matter how great or insightful my stay is at a hotel or resort, I still feel that home sweet home is special. I never have a feeling of sadness that others have when saying a final goodbye to a wonderful vacation or hotel stay, nor do I feel dread that I'm heading home . . . no matter *how* nice my visit was. That's because I have designed my home to be my special, favorite place. And I believe that your home can—and should—be this for you, too! If you can't say that your home is your favorite place to be, I encourage you to start taking action to get it there. Your home is often where the most precious moments of your life unfold with family and friends, a place where you spend a significant part of your life, so why not dedicate the time, energy, and resources to make it worthy of that?

I want this book to help you create a home that, *relaxes*, *reenergizes*, and *restores* you (my three Rs), starting the moment you walk through the front door. Home sweet home should be your safe place, one that makes your heart sing. Your home can match any five-star resort when it comes to a feeling of deep comfort and happiness, and it can rival the finest hotel because it will be personal and reflective of all that is special about *you* and *your experiences*. Sadly, for too many of us, that's simply not the case because our houses aren't designed or organized for our emotional and physical well-being.

One of the ideas that always resonates when I talk to groups, large and small, is that we are in total control of the "messaging" in our homes. Objects, colors, furniture arrangement, the number of things we own, and how they are organized (or not) tells a story not only to guests but to *you*. When you walk into your home, what message do you want to receive from it? For me, the message is warmth, comfort, order, and happiness. It says, "Welcome home. Kick off your shoes (and place them out of sight, of course) and settle in." I think most of us want to feel this way when we come home—but if the hall closet is bulging, the table is strewn with clutter, and you have no designated place to stow your keys or place your mail, coming home can feel chaotic and uneasy.

To achieve the three Rs in your home, let's think strategically and carefully about what we choose to fill spaces (fine hotels and resorts do this, too). Oftentimes, we buy something as a temporary placeholder, or because it's on sale, or because we feel we need something and we settle for "just okay" or "it will have to do." I've done this myself. There were times when I wished I had resisted the temptation to buy something not quite right because it filled a space or a need. Now I know that it's better to try to wait and to not fill the space until the perfect item comes along. I've also learned to resist purchasing something because it's a phenomenal deal and I like it. I have to truly need it or love it. Today there isn't anything in my home that I regret having—but it took time for me to achieve that. Another lesson I've learned is that eventually

the right item *does* come along—and it's always worth waiting for.

I understand that you may not have the resources to acquire the perfect furnishings and accessories right away, but that doesn't mean you should buy something that's not quite right. Learning the hard way, I have found it is wiser to live with what I have, or live with the empty space, and save up for the right item. Sometimes, there's simply no choice because function dictates need (you probably don't want to sit on the floor in your living room!). I get that. For those times, spend as little as you can, for as much quality as you can get, to allow you to save up for the eventual, perfect thing.

That said, as much as I love my home, I also appreciate a well-designed and well-appointed hotel room just as much as you probably do. When clients tell me that they want their bedroom or bathroom to look like a luxury hotel room or a fabulous resort spa, I understand exactly what they want because these places exude a quality of relaxation and calm. What *is* that quality? It's not the aesthetics of a hotel room or spa bathroom, which are fairly generic even in high-end properties. Rather, it's the *tranquility* these spaces provide that people find so magical.

We love hotels and resorts because things tend to be in order, and there is minimal visual clutter to interfere with the pleasure of being away. In many cases, their aesthetic choices may not even be that extraordinary—actually, even fine resorts make nonpersonal design decisions, meant to appeal to and serve many different kinds of people. Independent of the design style, we are reacting to the cleanliness, simplicity, and order of the space. And of course, we're consciously free of the burdens of maintenance. These qualities conspire to let us breathe and think, relax and restore. Great resorts and hotels all use common strategies that we can implement in our own homes and are tailored to work for our day-to-day lives and our styles. I've adapted many of these resort principles into my own homes, and those of my clients, to help re-create that relaxed sense of being on vacation every time that home is entered. They are principles I share with

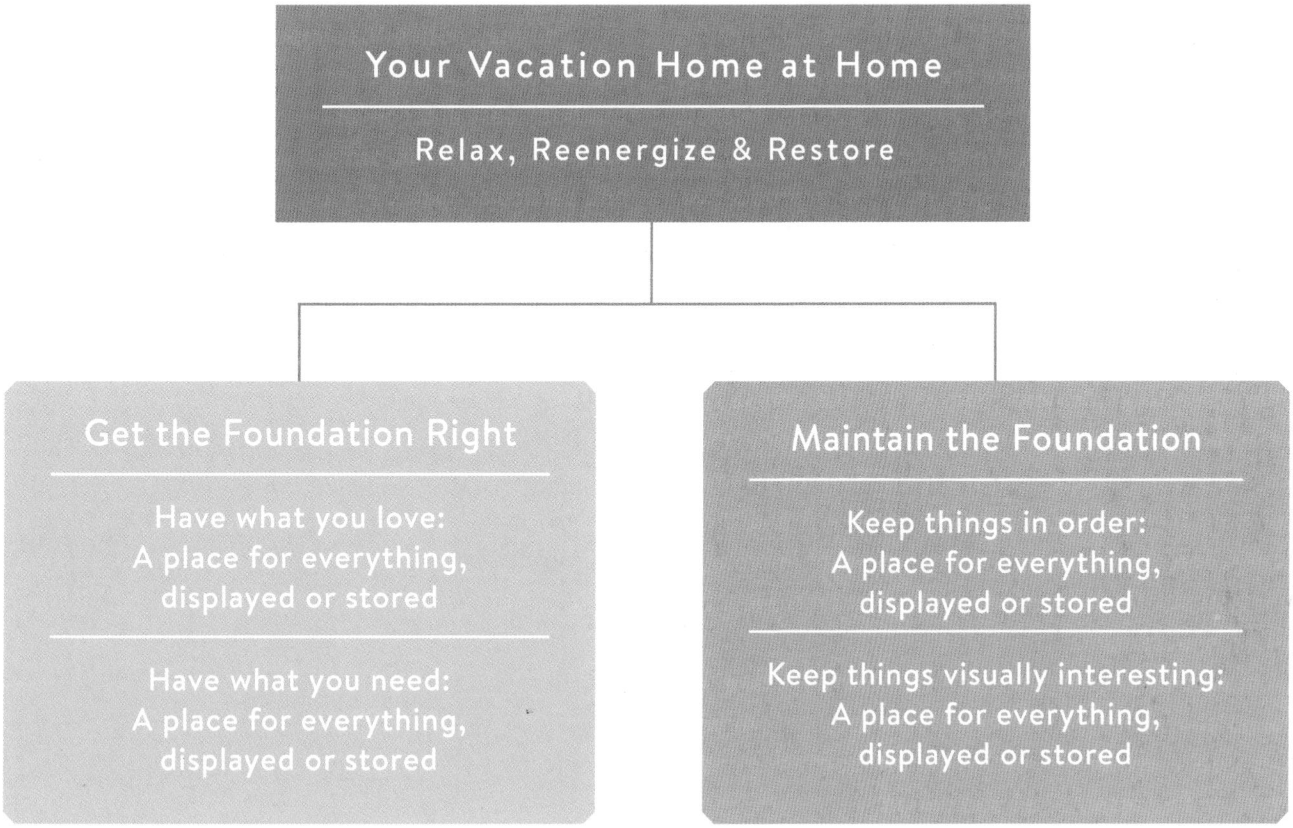

Your Vacation Home at Home

Relax, Reenergize & Restore

Get the Foundation Right

Have what you love:
A place for everything,
displayed or stored

Have what you need:
A place for everything,
displayed or stored

Maintain the Foundation

Keep things in order:
A place for everything,
displayed or stored

Keep things visually interesting:
A place for everything,
displayed or stored

you in this book and that I reiterate throughout because I want to drive home the point that your ultimate retreat is right at your doorstep.

I truly believe that you can achieve a "vacation at home" with my clear, concrete strategies for design and maintenance, and combine them with your personal collections, favorite colors, and lifestyle. I promise it's doable, and it's *so* worth the effort to create a neat and beautifully personal home that allows each object, accessory, and piece of furniture in it to shine.

This is only half the battle, though. The other half is maintaining that vacation-like feel so that each time you walk through your front door, you are instantly relaxed, reenergized, and restored. When our homes are tidy and free of distraction, we are generally more productive, and we discover we have more time to enjoy our family, friends, and favorite pursuits. You can do it, too, and I show you how.

Once you have the right solutions, and a simple system in place to implement them during the course of a normal day, you'll see that having a beautiful, tidy home becomes second nature. You will never have to scramble to pick up minutes (or seconds!) before a friend drops by unexpectedly. Throwing a party can be an impromptu event instead of a dreaded obligation that takes weeks of cleaning and planning.

In part 1, "There's No Place Like Home," I take you through the philosophy of transforming your everyday home into a relaxing vacation home, borrowing many ideas from fine resort and hotel design.

In part 2, "Everyday Vacation Home Room by Room," we take a closer look at each kind of room in your house. While the general principles discussed in part 1 apply to every room, each room in a home also has unique features—kitchens have cooking equipment, and bathrooms have showers or baths. Living rooms often have large furniture not found in home offices or in a kitchen. In chapter 3, "Living and Dining," chapter 4, "Sleeping and Bathing," and chapter 5, "At Work and Play," I talk about the many ways we can add delight to individual spaces

through design choices that help reinforce the resort idea and help invigorate for what lies ahead, and unwind at the end of a busy and productive day. Throughout, I help you figure out how to keep what you've got neat and orderly and looking great. No, it's not the household hints section; it's an important discussion about how to keep what you've created working on your behalf and serving your needs and the needs of your family and friends. Your home should work for you; you shouldn't have to be a slave to your surroundings.

You may notice that important advice is sometimes repeated. This is done intentionally as a way of making this book easy and convenient to use; I don't want you to have to search for information if you are just focusing on one particular space. For example, I want you to find all the bathroom information in the section on bathrooms. However, I also want you to be aware of the same information if you are just beginning your design journey and reading the overview chapters. I often find that being reminded of key points, exactly where they're applicable, helps illuminate the overall goal and proves helpful for committing them to memory!

Part 3, "Everyday Vacation Homes Up Close," highlights four homes that truly exemplify vacation living at home. The first is my new, personal project in Rosemary Beach, Florida, which consists of a main house and an efficiently designed carriage house capable of operating independently as a small home for a family of four. After designing and building our first home in Rosemary Beach in 2014, I thought that it would be our forever beach home. Never say forever! After a confluence of events, we decided to sell the house and renovate another one in the same town. That's one of the projects you'll meet here. Since the main home is a place where my husband and I, our children, and our dogs go to unwind and spend precious family time together, it was important that the rooms exuded a resort feel while holding up to high-energy kids and pets, visits to the beach, and weekend guests. Yet it still had to be personal and reflective of our tastes, interests, travels, and needs.

The next two homes are places I designed for clients in Utah using all the ideas you'll find in this book. One of these homes is based in the desert of St. George and has the benefit of dramatic views and vistas of the surrounding Red Rocks. The other home is located in Park City, a fairly renowned ski and outdoor sport town. It has to hold up to the comings and goings of skiers and snowboarders, so withstanding the functional needs of the client, in addition to their aesthetic preferences was particularly crucial. The owners and I made sure that the interior spaces took advantage of the natural surroundings to inspire and rejuvenate. Finally, my small carriage house in Rosemary Beach demonstrates how cozy spaces can live large, with plenty of storage, and still exude a sense of relaxation and calm. It's a perfect place for guests to unwind when they visit—it's relaxing and comfortable, and it still reflects a resort feeling. And though we primarily use it for guests, our family of four has lived in it quite comfortably for extended periods of time.

When I began to think about writing this book, I was inspired by something the late Steve Jobs once said:

"Your time is limited, so don't waste it living someone else's life."

Similarly, we shouldn't waste our lives living in someone else's idea of the perfect home—or feeling as if we must run away to a resort or vacation home to escape our everyday environment. There is no need to do either of these things when you have an everyday vacation home! Of course, you should travel and explore, and rent a vacation home if you want, but there should be no place like home. What I want you, my readers, to take away from *Vern Yip's Vacation at Home* are the tools and strategies to tailor your home to you so that it receives you warmly, relaxes you immediately, and rejuvenates you always so that you can live *your* life every day in the spot *you* love most on the planet!

PART 1

THERE'S NO PLACE LIKE HOME

There are two main objectives to accomplish in order to have a "vacation at home"—first, create spaces that are serene and uncluttered, and second, use strategies that make them easy to keep that way. Both can be accomplished no matter what your personal aesthetic. I've enjoyed oasis-like homes that were beachy and relaxed in neutral tones, and those that were boldly masculine with lots of leather and wood. The beauty of creating your vacation home *at home* is that the strategies work with any interior design style. By making style and design choices that are beautiful, functional, and ultrasimple to organize, important papers, appliances, and any objects and items you don't want on display are also easily within reach. Maintaining your environment with a minimum of effort and time means choosing materials and furnishings that make tidying up a breeze but that also always look pleasing to the eye.

CHAPTER 1

CREATE THE PERFECT ENVIRONMENT

Like many of you, I am busy with family and work, so the only way I can stay sane is if my house is attractive, organized, and clean. If I had to deal with distress and craziness in my own space, I don't think I'd be productive or happy. My rooms, indoors and out, need to rejuvenate and recharge me, and my interest in making sure my house is easy to maintain stems from that. I also try to create that feeling for my clients in their homes—beautiful design is great, but it also has to provide function.

This doesn't mean you have to minimize to an unrealistic degree. I am certainly not a minimalist; I love beautiful things! But when you have so many things everywhere, rooms become oppressive. Worse, you become blind to individual objects that you may have once appreciated but that have since become muted by the clutter around them. Clutter, and other visual distractions in a space, can lead to feeling stressed. The minimalist movement is partially propelled by the idea that less translates to more sanity. In many cases, though, I feel minimalism can take things too far.

Getting rid of all our possessions can create bare, cold environments that often feel restrictive to live in after a while, and that can bring on stress, too. The key, then, becomes finding the perfectly calibrated balance that's tailored for you and your family where you are surrounded by the things that you need and love, where those things have a designated space to live in where they both breathe and can be appreciated, and where you can be visually stimulated in a positive way. The aim is finding a balance and creating beautifully edited rooms that highlight individual objects in a way that creates a pleasing whole.

For instance, I want to show off my children's artwork, but I don't want my fridge covered with bright magnets or tape holding up a multitude of crayon and finger-paint pictures. For me, this display method doesn't celebrate the work my children put into creating something unique the way that I would like, nor does it contribute to the cleanliness and orderliness of my kitchen. When my son, Gavin, or daughter, Vera, brings a creative project home from school, I want to show it off and give it the recognition I feel it deserves. My solution is to elevate the "artwork of the month" either in a nice frame or, if it's a 3-D object, on a pedestal. Why not award a place of honor to the things (and people) we cherish? Personally speaking, I think it's preferable to placing something on a handy surface, where it just becomes an addition to the overall clutter rather than an object worthy of attention. And in doing so, everyone,

the family and guests alike, can ooh and aah over Gavin's and Vera's efforts. This makes my children feel encouraged and helps promote and develop further artistic endeavors.

I love the quirky, personal items that give a home character. There is every reason to live with the little things that make us happy. Any kind of collection can be organized and displayed in a beautiful way. A room stripped of everything but the necessities lacks personality and warmth. No one wants to live in a furniture showroom. In real life, we have stuff. While your stuff should be either meaningful or necessary or both, the real trick is in arranging it in a convenient and aesthetically pleasing way.

Remember, too, that the rules of design and organization shouldn't have to change just because you have a small space or budget. Buy the highest-quality items that you can afford—the benefit of doing this is that you will naturally buy fewer things and those items will last. Ask yourself, *What do I need and what do I love?* Be sure to take your time building on the answers to those questions, especially if you're on a budget. Also ask, *Is it special enough?* before you pull the trigger. I've learned that just because something is on sale, or purchased at a great value, isn't a reason to buy it. No matter the size of your wallet, always keep aesthetics in mind when selecting functional objects. My experience is that you get the most bang for your buck by making sure necessary items, such as lighting fixtures, are truly reflective of your style and taste. That way, you're essentially getting two things for the price of one—art *and* illumination.

As I've said, I am not a minimalist, but there are many parts of the movement that I embrace, especially the recognition that simplifying is not about deprivation but about creating more space (literal and psychological) for living and loving. When we have fewer things that demand our attention—five pillows to fluff instead of twenty-five, or six really beautiful coffee mugs to organize instead of thirty mediocre ones—we have more time to experience life. That's another reason why we feel relaxed at a resort:

we're not spending time managing an overflow of often meaningless possessions as much as we are outside the room, experiencing new adventures and interacting with the local culture. Your home can give you that freedom, too, and in fact, I think it should. You owe it to yourself.

To that end, there are eighteen primary rules or strategies you can use to create a resort-like vacation at home, every day. I come back to reflect on this list throughout the book because I want to emphasize these points and demonstrate how they work throughout the house. They are:

1. TELL THE STORY.
2. CREATE A GREAT FIRST IMPRESSION.
3. HAVE A FOCAL POINT.
4. USE SYMMETRY.
5. DESIGN FOR THE SENSES.
6. REFRESH THE VISUAL.
7. RESET THE SPACE.
8. SPACE PLAN.
9. USE FEWER THINGS BUT BIGGER THINGS.
10. CONSIDER MONOCHROMATIC PALETTES.
11. KEEP WHAT YOU LOVE AND WHAT YOU NEED.
12. TAKE ADVANTAGE OF CLOSED STORAGE (OR CONTAINERS WITH LIDS).
13. ELEVATE WHAT YOU LOVE AND DISPLAY PROPERLY.
14. SHOWCASE LOW-MAINTENANCE ORGANICS.
15. INSTALL DIMMERS WHERE POSSIBLE.
16. INCORPORATE THE COLOR WHITE.
17. INVEST IN QUALITY.
18. SMARTLY MINIMIZE YOUR TO-DO LIST.

1. **TELL THE STORY.** Create a personal narrative by using things you want to see. Top resorts and hotels work overtime to ensure that you are only surrounded by positive messaging when you first arrive and when you see your room for the first time. You can do the same thing in your own home.

2. **CREATE A GREAT FIRST IMPRESSION.** No matter how small your home may be, it's important to be warmly and calmly greeted when you first enter it by a foyer or thoughtful entrance sequence. The entrance sets the tone for your home, so spend the time and energy to create a positive first and last impression.

3. **HAVE A FOCAL POINT.** Every room should have a clear focus whether that's a view, fireplace, soaking tub, or large-scale piece of art. Your eye needs to know where to logically land so that it's not constantly and uncomfortably darting around the space.

4. **USE SYMMETRY.** This is a great organizing and design device. It helps establish an order that we, as humans, are used to seeing. After all, we have even been designed to be symmetrical. It's a part of the natural world (think snowflakes, honeycombs, and so on); therefore, it makes sense that it's calming and soothing for us to enter into environments that are largely symmetrical. Most people understand symmetry to be identical, or very closely identical, items facing each other or pointed toward a central axis point (e.g., a fireplace, flat-screen television, view). In design, symmetry also refers to a sense of harmonious and beautiful proportion and balance, which can help incorporate order into a space. I've often encouraged clients to purchase items in pairs so that they can institute symmetry more easily in their own homes!

5. **DESIGN FOR THE SENSES.** Smell, touch, and sound are just as important as sight (see box on page 11 for tips).

6. **REFRESH THE VISUAL.** Change things up to keep it exciting like a hotel does. Even if you're surrounded by things you love, your eye can't help but get used to what it sees on a daily basis. By switching things around occasionally, you'll better appreciate all your beloved items.

7. **RESET THE SPACE.** When you're done using a room, make it a habit to reset it so that the next time you enter it, it's ready to use and pleasant to look at. This includes making the bed, clearing the sink of dishes, and re-fluffing the sofa and throw pillows.

8. **SPACE PLAN.** Make sure to thoughtfully arrange your space to serve you in the best way possible. If it feels maxed out, try to pull an item or two out. Space can be the ultimate luxury and one of your most powerful tools for creating a calm, relaxing atmosphere. Top properties know this well and avoid packing every corner of their lobby or rooms with furniture and accessories.

9. **USE FEWER THINGS BUT BIGGER THINGS.** This will help minimize the visual clutter and help with clear messaging in the room. This applies to artwork, furniture, mirrors, light fixtures, and so on. Make sure these special items are also properly lit. It will help you appreciate them even more.

10. CONSIDER MONOCHROMATIC PALETTES. Limiting the number of colors applied to a space will help to relax the eye and mind. This is also true when thinking of open space–plan homes. Think of an entire floor plan as a single room in this case. Accent colors can always come in with artwork, accessories, and even furniture, but having a cacophony of colors applied to your room's walls can be difficult to live with long term and is not very calming.

11. KEEP WHAT YOU LOVE AND WHAT YOU NEED. Sell, donate, or dispose of the rest.

12. TAKE ADVANTAGE OF CLOSED STORAGE (OR CONTAINERS WITH LIDS). Ensure that you have plenty of closed storage to keep life's necessities handy but largely out of sight (think mail, keys, and leashes hidden away inside a lidded box, for example). Closed storage can also help you rotate your decorative items, by housing extra items out of sight, so that not everything you own is on display at the same time. Outside of closets and built-in cabinets, think about furniture pieces replete with opaque doors and drawers as well as lidded boxes and baskets.

13. ELEVATE WHAT YOU LOVE AND DISPLAY PROPERLY. Think like a museum and honor those items you choose to keep and want to be seen. Use platforms, pedestals, and book stacks to help elevate and display properly.

14. SHOWCASE LOW-MAINTENANCE ORGANICS. It's pretty impossible to substitute replicas for organic items (like fruit or plants) that connect a room's interior to nature and help set a relaxing tone. Therefore, choose items that require less upkeep and offer the most bang for the buck: orchid plants, bowls of apples, long-lasting cut flowers, and the like.

15. INSTALL DIMMERS WHERE POSSIBLE. These should be on every switch and every lamp in your home. It will be infinitely more calming to come home to softer lighting than to be blasted.

16. INCORPORATE THE COLOR WHITE. It signifies cleanliness, which puts your mind at ease. It's why hotels only use white sheets and white towels. But white can be used in many different ways throughout a home in bathroom and kitchen fixtures and appliances, on walls to give a gallery feel, and in furnishings and accessories. I read something I liked about the color white: "[It's] the Botox of paint colors . . . everything is younger and fresher for it."

17. INVEST IN QUALITY. It's important to purchase what you love and to purchase items that will last your lifetime. Be done with junky placeholders as soon as you can—though I know this is not achievable for anyone overnight. It may take years to reach this goal, but it really is worth the wait.

18. SMARTLY MINIMIZE YOUR TO-DO LIST. Select materials that will remove maintenance from your to-do list whenever possible: LED bulbs, quartz countertops, performance fabrics, nylon 6,6 carpet and rugs, evergreen bushes and plants, and so on. There is enough going on in most of our lives, so choose items that can begin to eliminate duties from your list.

THE SENSES AND RELAXING DESIGN

We tend to think primarily of how things look when we talk interior design, but don't neglect the other senses—namely, smell, touch, and sound!

SMELL. Make sure you're greeted by a clean, pleasant smell in your own home. Even the most beautiful environment can't overcome a bad odor, so ensure that you love the way it smells. Use your cooktop's ventilation system when preparing hot meals. Put shoes and dirty laundry away until you can clean them. Take household trash out each day and place it in a closed container outside. Change pet litter regularly. Finally, use high-quality home fragrance devices (candles, diffusers, reeds, and so on) to keep your home smelling pleasant and fresh. Your guests will thank you, too.

TOUCH. There are countless ways your body interacts with your home, and it's constantly taking cues from those interactions. Making informed decisions, tailored to how you want to feel in that space, is critical in helping facilitate pleasurable and relaxing physical interactions with your home. It is just as important as making selections that will appeal to you visually. For example, in addition to absorbing sound, having a soft rug or carpet for your feet to land on softens your exit out of bed in the morning. Selecting a material that you love sitting on, in addition to selecting one that is practical for the way you live your life, is incredibly important when it comes to, say, picking out a sofa. A velvet sofa will feel a lot different from a linen one—so choose what feels best to you.

SOUND. What you hear (or don't hear) can impact how pleasurable it is to be in a space. Whether it's blissful quiet, the sound of music, or the sounds of nature (birds chirping, waves crashing on the shore, rain dripping off jungle leaves, or even a fountain bubbling with water), most of us need our ears to be pleased as well as our eyes and noses when we're trying to relax. Many high-end hotels have a musical track on when you enter a room, to transport you immediately to a more relaxing place. This trick is easier to duplicate than ever with the advent of digital music. If music helps you relax, create a digital music playlist and invest in a Bluetooth speaker (for as little as twenty dollars) as part of an accessible system that makes playing your music easy as soon as you enter your home. Sometimes quiet is beautiful, too; if you're trying to muffle unwanted sound or just want the "sound of silence," make sure you incorporate rugs, drapes, and plenty of other soft surfaces to help absorb those intrusive noises. If you live in the city and pine for peace, consider a white noise machine that muffles unpleasant sounds while blending into the background, offering a relaxing and—after a while—unnoticeable hum.

MINIMALISM VERSUS RESTRAINT

My work has often been described as architectural and sometimes even "minimalist." I would rather describe what I do as "clean-lined but warm." I love to delight and surprise with a pop of color, dramatic artwork, or a unique object that sets the tone for a room. These items let you know where to focus in a space, which immediately puts you in a more relaxed frame of mind. I was particularly struck by the distinction between *clean-lined* and *minimalist* when I started reading about the minimalist movement. There is a lot to admire about the philosophy of paring down to bare essentials, but I personally could not live with so little, and I think it's challenging for others as well.

For me, paring down means only having the things around you that you really love, have true personal meaning, and serve your needs, either functionally or emotionally. It's also about restraint—not overstuffing a room with more than it needs. This is a practice that I have to regularly apply in my own home. For as long as I can remember, I have been a magnet for hardcover books. Books layer a room with soul and inspire so much of my work, so I have select ones placed in virtually every room of the house in addition to the stacks on my bookshelves. Not only do I love how they look on a side table, coffee table, or console, but I also love being able to quickly peruse one on my way from one part of the house to another.

However, if I'm not careful, the inflow of new books could quickly make my soulful rooms look claustrophobic. So once a year, I'll quickly comb through my books. Once a month, I rotate the books out on display with the shelved ones as a refresh of the space. If a table feels like it could accommodate one or two more books, I'll stop short of adding them to allow for the critical breathing space.

Restraint is about having the things you honestly want and need—and not one thing more. It is also about choosing a timeless color scheme that helps you relax, connecting throughout adjoining spaces. It's about proportions and dimensions that maximize the feeling of ease and comfort within a space, and it is keeping clutter tucked away behind closed storage.

I learned the closed storage lesson before I was ten years old in a very interesting way. From the time I could pick up a pencil, my mother noticed that I had a penchant for design. Unlike most of my peers, I was never enthralled by team sports or video games. I could, however, easily entertain myself for countless hours by filling volumes of sketchbooks with drawings of homes and the furniture that would fill them. When I was seven, my mom encouraged me to design my own bedroom furniture and then actually had it made. This took place during a time in our lives when there wasn't a lot of extra money, so the fact that she dedicated resources to making my dream a reality is an incredible testament to her faith in me, even when I was so young.

I designed an all chrome-and-glass bedroom suite, with towers of open shelving flanking either side of my twin bed and a bridge with even more open shelving connecting their tops. It was exactly what I wanted aesthetically and helped set the sparse, modern tone I had been longing to have! But, boy, was it hard to keep clean and uncluttered. Rather than the closed storage that could have hidden all my stuff and given me that uber-clean-lined room that I was after, I was stuck constantly trying to figure out how to get my necessary but unattractive stuff out of sight, and keeping all those open shelves looking nice and uncluttered became a burden. It didn't take me long to realize that open-glass shelving needed almost constant straightening, polishing, and dusting! Not a vacation, especially for a seven-year-old.

IT'S WHAT YOU DON'T SEE THAT MATTERS

When walking into a well-run luxury resort, the first thing I notice is an organized and visually delightful lobby area—an orderly reception desk, a smartly dressed clerk, perhaps a floral arrangement or an overscaled accessory, a welcoming seating group, and maybe a beautifully framed painting or photograph. That's it. What's more important is what you *don't* see. No stacks of mail, no piles of receipts. No bowls of paper clips, no printers, multiline telephones, or any of the other necessary but unappealing clutter that it takes to run a business. The first step in achieving that luxury-resort look and feel is to visualize the end point: an environment that expertly shows off your loved items without the distraction of your necessary but unattractive stuff.

In the chapters to follow, I review all the ways we can make our homes beautiful and organized, but here are some basics of good design that can help you get started.

• KEEP THINGS MOVING

Hotels and resorts are high-traffic areas, although often you'd never know it. That's because the lobby and other public spaces are designed to keep people flowing freely, and furniture is arranged so as not to impede that flow. There's nothing worse than entering a room and not being able to figure out how to easily get to the other end. Don't block doorways with furniture. Make sure there is a visible path around the room. Give people at least thirty-six inches for pathways between areas and at least twenty-four inches between pieces of furniture.

• TOSS IT, STORE IT, REPOSITION IT

Still keeping your hotelier's hat on, mentally divide your stuff into three piles. The first, pile 1, contains the stuff that brightens your day, the stuff you look forward to looking at. These are the props you'll use to set the stage for your luxurious retreat. We'll come back to them. Pile 2 is the stuff you need to conduct the business of your life (organize it in a folder, a drawer, a closet), and stuff you need to have around but can't hide (keep it where it's least likely to interfere with the focal points you create for each space within your home). Pile 3 is everything you don't need at all—so toss, sell, or donate it.

• IF YOU LOVE IT, LEAVE IT

Display only things that you truly love and that speak to you, and give them a place of honor in your home. It's important to give them visual breathing room to be appreciated. If you have more loved items than you can properly display in the space that you have, properly store some out of sight and rotate showcasing them rather than overcrowding your rooms.

• CURATE THE THINGS YOU LOVE

Restraint has a mantra: you *can* have too much of a good thing. That doesn't mean, though, that you can't be a collector of beautiful objects. Allow items to command center stage on a shelf, mantel, or side table with plenty of storage. Trays are great for assembling smaller items and keeping things organized and neat in appearance. They also help to draw your eye to your most important possessions by underscoring them. Presented on their own, things look singularly special. Purposefully display accessories, objects, and collections on pedestals or plinths (these display supports are readily available online and through many retailers) to elevate their presence and their importance in your life. Even a neat stack of books can serve as a plinth for a treasured accessory. By displaying these items as if they were in a museum or art gallery, you highlight the qualities that drew you to them in the first place.

Don't be afraid to change things up on occasion. I especially like to do this with the decorative objects that adorn my foyer table and have the important job of greeting me each time I come home. They're first-impression objects, so I make sure to rotate through appropriately scaled travel treasures that fondly remind me of special trips. And changing out just one significant object in a space can completely refresh a room's look and feel.

It's normal for your eye to get accustomed to seeing things in their usual places, so make changes to give yourself a nice visual delight. That's another reason why hotels and resorts can energize us so much: there's always something new and exciting to engage with. If, for instance, you have twenty vases in your pottery collection, how about showing off three or five at a time, rotating the collection monthly, keeping the others tucked safely behind closed storage? This way, you're continuously reminded that your collection consists of many different objects of beauty, and that each one is an individual jewel, not just part of an unwieldly group.

Turn a specified area, shelf, side table, niche, or mantel into a shrine to something meaningful—like a favorite travel memento or something your kid made, but try to refrain from overdoing it. By limiting the number of objects on these surfaces, you give them room to breathe and to be displayed properly so that they convey extreme value even if these objects don't have high monetary worth. Pausing to enjoy something meaningful and beautiful can be restorative.

For example, I have a series of different-colored ceramic cups our son Gavin made in the first grade. To honor their significance, I made a little plinth for all the cups to sit on. This placement treats the cups as the works of art they are to me, and, by positioning them the way a gallery would, others can see their beauty through my eyes.

• MIX IT UP

Mixing in uniquely handcrafted, vintage, and antique pieces with new and mass-produced pieces is important for grounding a room and giving it a patina that takes the edge off a room design. When everything is new, it can look contrived, stiff, and impersonal.

• IDENTIFY A FOCAL POINT

As I said earlier, focal points are important, and every room can have one. Once you know your focal point—whether it's a window with a view, a fireplace mantel, or a feature wall with interesting art—build seating around it and place objects so that they complement and not compete with it.

• OPEN IT UP

Plan your furniture arrangement so that when you enter the room, you immediately know where the seating areas are and how to reach them. In other words, don't block the view or path in the room by placing a sofa in front of the entryway. The back of a sofa works like a visual wall and prevents an easy flow through the space. Never place the back of a sofa in front of a fireplace opening. Instead, consider a daybed, lounge, or pair of chairs that allow you to visually connect with the fire.

• WATCH OUT

Thankfully, today's televisions are unobtrusive. Instead of the big bulky boxes of the past, sleek screens are discreet and often quite stylish in an understated way. No reason to hide them away in old-fashioned TV cabinets and oversized armoires. Make sure you place televisions only in rooms where you will actually watch them, and place furniture in a way that viewers can face them easily and enjoy the show. Also, keep in mind media content is no longer exclusively received via televisions; more people are now taking in their programming via laptops and other electronic devices. So really ask yourself whether an actual television is necessary in a space.

• LAYER IT

If your sofa is floating in the space, as opposed to sitting up against a wall, consider placing a sofa table, console, buffet, or other piece of long and low furniture behind it. This creates a more finished and more interesting look, and helps avoid the feeling of unintentionally walking "behind the scenes."

• DEFINE AREAS

Rugs can be helpful when you're trying to establish areas in multipurpose rooms. When determing the size of rug for a room, make sure that at least the two front legs of all the seating furniture sit on the rug comfortably. Typically, a rug should be sized so that there is a twelve- to eighteen-inch border all the way around the rug to the limiting-room condition, whether that's a wall or some other factor, such as a fireplace hearth or bump out.

• INTRODUCE SOFT ELEMENTS

Remember to install soft elements, such as floor-to-ceiling drapes and throw pillows, to help with sound absorption and to help visually soften a space. The important thing to remember, with drapery, is not to skimp on width or length. Oftentimes, decorative panels are too skinny to functionally cover a window in closed position. Even though those panels may *never* be pulled closed, it's still important to have their widths *look* like they will reasonably work.

> » Draperies should go as high as possible to the ceiling to eliminate visual breaks and let your eye travel seamlessly. There should only be a couple of inches of wall showing above the top of the drapery rod. This strategy offers the benefit of making ceilings appear higher and windows larger.

> » Ensure your drapery hardware extends at least three to four inches beyond the outside of the window frame and at least four to six above the trim—or as high as one to two inches below the ceiling.

> » Minimize light gaps, maximize privacy, and add a luxurious look by adding an extra four to five inches of fabric to each window panel.

> » To make narrow windows appear wider, add extra fabric to the overall drapery panel width. The fabric should cover the window frame, exposing only the glass.

> » Accent pillows, throws, and rugs are other soft elements that help to create a calm, restorative atmosphere. Like drapery, these key pieces assist with sound absorption, while also lending texture and color. They contribute to a more relaxed, vacation-like atmosphere. A word of caution when adding decorative throw pillows—practice restraint. Too many can make seating unusable or awkward, so consider going with fewer to keep the function up and the clutter down.

● INCORPORATE ORGANIC COMPONENTS

Throughout high-end hotel and resort properties, you see small containers filled with fruit, green plants, orchids, and, of course, arranged flowers. These visual—and often scented—touches evoke nature and its ability to soothe and calm. Hotels have large, dedicated budgets to these kinds of elements, but most homeowners have to get by with far fewer resources. Keep in mind that many cut flowers last, on average, only about five to seven days. To adorn your home with beautiful flowers and greenery for less money and effort, seek out low-maintenance plants and longer-lasting cut flowers (see the adjacent chart for a list of my favorite cut flowers and how long they last). Putting out beautiful displays of fruit is also a hallmark of a great resort. This can also be achieved at home economically if you choose the right fruit to showcase. Some fruits, such as apples, can last longer in an unattended bowl than others. A bag of Granny Smith or Red Delicious apples can be had for less than three dollars in many places.

» Use bud vases on your bathroom vanities, next to kitchen sinks, and on nightstands.

» Orchids are elegant, simple, and easy to take care of. They're also the most economical way to have fresh flowers in your home. A healthy orchid with plenty of buds, placed in bright, indirect sunlight, can produce blooms for eight to nine weeks and can cost under fifteen dollars per plant.

» Using single stems in multiple vases throughout a home affords a pulled-together look that can add a feeling of tranquility.

» A single flower type, used in multiples, makes a memorable arrangement that's easy to accomplish without a professional.

» Allowing a few stems to breathe in a larger vase, so that they can be truly appreciated, brings understated drama.

CHOOSE CUT FLOWERS WISELY

FLOWER	COLOR	LIFE SPAN
Anthodium	red, pink, green	up to six weeks
Cymbidium Orchid	various	up to six weeks
Dianthus	green	up to four weeks
Hydrangea	various	up to three weeks
Star of Bethlehem	white, orange, yellow	up to three weeks
Protea	various	up to three weeks
Carnation	various	up to three weeks
Alstroemeria	various	up to two weeks
Craspedia	yellow	up to two weeks
Chrysanthemum	various	up to two weeks
Daisy	various	up to two weeks
Rose	various	up to two weeks
Phalaenopsis	various	up to two weeks
Oncidium Orchid	various	up to two weeks

• FURNITURE PLACEMENT

In my first book, *Design Wise*, I spent a great deal of time on the right measurements for furniture, fixture, and art and accessory placement and scale. However, I think it is worth repeating some basic numbers here to keep in mind as you read this book and implement its ideas.

» 18 INCHES: Distance between coffee table and sofa.

» ½ TO ⅔ SOFA LENGTH: The ideal length for a corresponding coffee table. An 8-foot sofa, for example, should have a corresponding coffee table that is no less than 4' long but no greater than 5'-4" long.

» 12 INCHES: Distance between lounge chair and dedicated ottoman.

» 24 INCHES: Distance between centerline of dining chairs.

» 24 INCHES: Minimum passage distance between furniture pieces.

» 36 INCHES: Ideal passage distance between furniture pieces and through a room.

» 12 TO 18 INCHES: Distance between rug edge and closest wall, fireplace hearth, or bump out.

» 2 INCHES: Minimum planning distance between directly adjacent furniture pieces or between furniture placed against a wall.

» 42 TO 120 INCHES: Minimum to maximum distance between seating pieces for ideal conversation.

» 1.5 TO 2.5 X SCREEN SIZE: Distance between the primary viewing area and your 1080p television. Seating for a 46" screen, for example, should be placed somewhere between 69" to 115" from the face of the screen.

• LIGHTING

Lighting—whether it's the right kind of recessed lighting, the perfect hanging fixture, or a great table or floor lamp—is imperative in creating a vacation feeling at home, yet it's often an overlooked component of design. Lighting should not be an afterthought! Warm, soft lighting creates a sense of ease—and is also flattering. Task lighting at desks and work areas (both in-room and out) is brighter but still warm white, which is easy on the eyes. The soft glow of landscape lighting lets us see where to go without being harsh and unpleasant. In short, lighting has to work for us; we need to see what we are doing when we're in the kitchen chopping and sautéing, and we need the right light to read and write by when we are working at home or just scanning the daily news reports on whatever device we use, whether it's an old-fashioned newspaper or the internet. Most of all, I think well-lit rooms are beautiful rooms. Natural light provides a cheerful backdrop for daytime activities, and soft ambient light provides a warmth, coziness, and romance for evening events, from a family dinner to a large celebration.

BULB	SAVES ENERGY	DIMMABLE	COLOR(S)
Incandescent		●	S, B, D
Compact fluorescent	●		S, B, D
Halogen		●	B, D
MR-16	●	●	B, D
Light-emitting diode (LED)	●	●	S, B, D
COLORS			
Soft/warm white: subdued, yellowish tone			S
Bright/cool white: brighter than soft, bluish tone			B
Daylight: brightest light, closest to natural			D

SELECT THE RIGHT LED BULBS

Even though LED lighting has been on the market now for several years, many people still struggle with selecting the correct LED light bulb to replace their existing incandescent (old-style) light bulbs. Now, with all the choices available, how can you make the right decision? Before LED technology became mainstream, words like *color temperature, lumens, color rendering index (CRI), beam spread,* and *efficacy* were unknown and unnecessary to consumers because bulb choice was so limited. Today, we can all be lighting and bulb experts if we just familiarize ourselves with this new vocabulary. Many of us want the same warm look and feel that traditional light bulbs provided, but we just don't know how to find it. The following guidance provides an easy way to choose the correct LED light bulb to meet your needs.

HERE IS THE STANDARD LIGHT BULB SHAPE MOST ARE FAMILIAR WITH:

This is an A19 light bulb. Before, this came in many wattage choices from 25 watts to 120 watts. All you knew was this was what you needed for your nightstand light fixture. You also already knew how much brighter a 100-watt light bulb was than a 40-watt light bulb. You simply went to your local store and purchased a light bulb. Now you walk into your local home improvement center and are presented with a myriad of different choices for the same-shaped light bulb.

I hope there is an expert in the aisle, because if not, you run the risk of once again choosing the wrong bulb and telling all your friends how much you dislike

LED because they look blue! What you didn't know is they look blue because you purchased a 5000 Kelvin (color temperature) light bulb since it was on sale and, therefore, the least expensive on the shelf. Traditional old-style light bulbs did not have color temperature choices, but generally the color temperature they emitted was between 2400 Kelvin and 3000 Kelvin. They also became warmer in color temperature when dimmed. When buying an LED bulb, look for those with a color temperature between 2400 and 3000 Kelvin for the most familiar glow to that of a traditional, incandescent bulb. Most find it to be the most comfortable and flattering, and I agree.

The following table can help you make the quick-and-easy light bulb choices for your home. This chart matches the current equal wattage from a traditional incandescent light bulb to an LED one. As LED efficiencies continue to improve, they will allow more lumens per watt. This chart helps you see the current equal wattages regardless of the shape of the bulb.

	TRADITIONAL LIGHT BULB	LED EQUIVALENT 2400K TO 2700K—COLOR TEMPERATURE
	 Incandescent or Halogen Bulb	 LED Bulb

WATTAGE COMPARISON

40 to 60 watts	5 to 8 watts
60 to 75 watts	7 to 10 watts
75 to 100 watts	7 to 15 watts
100 to 150 watts	15 to 20 watts

Incandescent Candelabra	LED Candelabra
25 watts	2 to 2.5 watts
40 watts	4 watts

BEFORE YOU CHECK OUT . . .

- **YOUR HOME SHOULD BE TAILORED TO YOU** to reflect your individual needs and personal style the way a custom suit or dress is tailored to your body.

- **DESIGN EACH SPACE TO FULFILL ITS PURPOSE,** using materials and elements that will make your life easier, more relaxed, and enjoyable.

- **INCORPORATE POSITIVE ELEMENTS THAT DELIGHT YOU** into your everyday environment.

- **DETERMINE THE FOCAL POINT** for each room. Every space has one.

- **ESTABLISH AN ORDER** to lend a sense of calm to a room.

- **FEWER BUT BIGGER** accessories help minimize visual clutter.

- **MONOCHROMATIC PALETTES** and a limited number of colors applied to a space help relax the eye and mind.

- **CLOSED STORAGE** ensures that you reduce distracting visual pollution and have a specific place for life's necessities and overflow items. You should have designated storage for mail, keys, office supplies, remote controls, leashes, and so on because this makes locating these items so much easier. Also, use closed, opaque storage to help you rotate your decorative items so that not everything you own has to be on display at the same time.

- **KEEP ONLY WHAT YOU LOVE** and what you need. Sell, donate, or dispose of the rest.

- **ELEVATE WHAT YOU LOVE** and display properly.

Think like a museum and honor those items you choose to keep and want to see. Use platforms, pedestals, and book stacks to help elevate and display properly.

- **GO ORGANIC.** It's pretty impossible to replace organic items with replicas, so choose items that require less upkeep and offer the most bang for the buck: orchids, bowls of apples or citrus, long-lasting cut flowers, tropical cut green leaves, and so on.

- **DIMMERS SHOULD BE ON EVERY SWITCH** and every lamp in your home.

- **WHITE IS POWERFUL** because it signifies cleanliness, which puts your mind at ease. It's why hotels only use white sheets and white towels.

- **BUY QUALITY** and what you love. It's important to purchase what you love and to purchase quality items that will last your lifetime. Be done with placeholders as soon as you can. It's not achievable for anyone overnight. It can take years, but a plan to get there keeps you on track.

- **SMARTLY MINIMIZE YOUR TO-DO LIST** and select materials that will remove maintenance from your to-do list whenever possible: LED bulbs, quartz countertops, performance fabrics, nylon 6,6 carpet and rugs, evergreen bushes and plants, and so on. There is enough going on in most of our lives, so choose items that can begin to eliminate duties from your list.

CHAPTER 2
FUNCTION MEETS AESTHETICS

Let's try a thought experiment. Go to your front door. Close your eyes and call to mind the sense of joy, ease, and relaxation you experience when you walk into a great resort property, rental home, or hotel room. Even if you've never been to one—or one that you love—imagine what you would hope to see, hear, smell, and touch. Now, open your eyes and look around. Is what you're seeing even better and more pleasing to the eye? Do you get that same feeling of calm and delight? When you walk into your own home, you should feel that same *ahh* moment, but an even better one because you have entered a space that is all yours, filled with *your* treasures and *your* favorite luxuries. For me, it's the sight of my family (both humans and canines), white Phaleonopsis orchids, the scent of lemongrass, the sound of classical music, and seeing a rotating selection of the artisan objects, collected from my journeys all over the world, artfully displayed and with plenty of breathing room.

Maybe you don't immediately feel calm, comfortable, and visually delighted as soon as you walk into your home. Instead, you experience feelings of chaos and disorganization, the nightmare opposites of tranquility and clarity. There are boots and shoes haphazardly lining the hallway; piles of mail on a console table; and handbags, briefcases, and knapsacks covering every available surface, including the floor. In short, you see all the clutter and mess of everyday life—exactly the stuff you are escaping when you seek out the refuge of a luxury hotel room.

Our little experiment demonstrates *why* we love that hotel-room look: it has none of the telltale reminders of the stresses of everyday life. Again, it's not so much *what* we see that draws us into that retreat; it's what we *don't* see. We are reacting to the cleanliness, simplicity, and uncluttered design and decor of those rooms.

As stated earlier, luxury resorts and hotels employ specific strategies to achieve this look and feel. Of course, they also have large staffs to address these things, whereas most households don't. Instead of using generic art and objects, we'll be using the things that *you* treasure, that are beautiful *to you*. The goal is to be visually delighted by what you see each time you enter your home. With the right details and elements in place, you can feel transported every time you walk into your home or a room in your home.

Maintaining this perfect environment is where the lessons from the minimalist movement really come into play. If clutter and disorganization are the enemies of relaxation, then extreme minimalism can feel like a soulless rejection of the things that make us unique individuals. For many people, a bare room without beloved touchstones and beautiful things to look at, feel, and smell creates its own form of stress. And though some in fact *do* find happiness living the minimalist lifestyle, many others (including me) feel that it's not realistic or sustainable in

the long run. If extreme minimalism isn't your style, consider my guidance as a middle ground that helps you adapt the principles of minimalism so they work for the way you and your family live your lives.

Each thing in your home carries a message, and those items work together to deliver an overall statement every time you enter a room. This is especially true for the first room you enter when you come home. Remember that this message is truly under your control. It can be "Welcome home! You were missed, so get ready to unwind and be nurtured," or "Hey, there's dirty laundry here for you to take care of, and be careful that you don't trip over all the shoes in the hallway. By the way, the light bulb above your head is still out." To change the messaging from an undesirable one to one that receives you pleasantly, you first need to get the foundation of your home right, and these three basic steps can help get you there:

1. Make an investment in the furniture and fixtures that work for you, providing you with all the function, support, and storage that's necessary.

2. Assign places to put your things and return them after you're finished with them.

3. Visually eliminate the things that you don't love and that deliver negative messaging.

High-end hotels and resorts really understand this power of messaging and how it affects a guest's all-important first impression. *Am I entering a soothing refuge, or am I just another road warrior who needs a place to flop for the night?* Many hotels can get this point wrong, with every surface in the room covered with stuff—a tray next to the TV with junk food and bottled water for sale; mini coffee machines with cups and capsules sitting on top of the dresser; the desk littered with marketing literature and magazines.

With all that stuff, you might as well be at home looking at your own clutter. So much for relaxing! But when you go into a high-end hotel room, the surfaces you see are blissfully bare—the snacks are inside a cabinet; the literature is in a binder in a desk drawer; and the carefully selected books and magazines have a clear, designated spot. Hoteliers understand that visual pollution is jarring, and they go to great lengths to keep rooms soothingly clutter-free so that guests are not assaulted by extraneous content. Taking a note from the minimalists, "less" can enhance relaxation more effectively than "more."

STORAGE SMARTS

When there is a place for everything and everything is in its place, your spaces are kept tidy and you don't have to waste time searching for needed items. Always make sure your method for storage works with the overall color palette and style of your room.

CLOSED STORAGE: Furniture with built-in closed storage, such as solid or frosted or mirrored glass door drawers and doors.

FOYER BOX: Use a closed, hinged box to accommodate car and house keys, mail, and even small dog leashes. These are great when you don't have a piece of furniture with built-in closed storage in the foyer or don't have room for something as substantial as a piece of furniture in your entryway.

MASON JARS: I keep a row of mason jars in the mudroom of my house to stow a variety of dog treats and dog toys. The jars look orderly and neat, but fun and whimsical, too—and the clear glass makes contents easy to identify.

BASKETS: In certain rooms, baskets can provide a neat place to stash children's toys (public rooms and children's bedrooms), neatly rolled towels and toiletries (bathroom), and extra blankets and pillows for overnight guests (guest room, living room if a pull-out sofa serves as guest quarters).

STORAGE OTTOMANS: Upholstered cubes and rectangles serve double duty as a place to sit or put your feet and keep larger items like toys and blankets out of sight but accessible.

REMOTE BOX: Stash all remote controls and other unsightly items you need at hand, like the latest book you're reading or your tablet, writing implements, aspirin, and so on.

MINIMIZE YOUR STRESS BY GETTING IT RIGHT THE FIRST TIME

It's not just "things" that distract the eye and jar the soul. What I call placeholders also do that. You didn't, or couldn't, make that initial investment in the right furniture, artwork, and accessories, so every day, those temporary placeholder pieces quietly remind you that you would ideally like to have something else. Make a plan to get rid of these placeholders. It doesn't have to happen overnight, but set a goal of surrounding yourself with quality pieces that will functionally service you and that you're visually enamored with—and you will find that you are rewarded by a steady stream of good, positive messages.

Setting a good foundation also happens by making sure everything you have actually works for you. The example of kitchen countertops illustrate what I mean. It stresses me to see things on the counter, even though I need to have them around. Like many people, my husband and I used to keep our knives in a block on the counter—knives are an essential part of kitchen equipment, of course—but the block was a blight on the clean, soothing lines of the countertop. We figured out a way to put the knives away in an easy-to-access knife drawer instead of a countertop block. Little things like this make looking at the kitchen more pleasant and calming. I like seeing clean countertops when I go to bed at night and again in the morning when I go down to the kitchen to start the day.

It's not just what you keep—or don't keep—on the kitchen counter that can make your life easier; it's the counter itself. Again, start with a good foundation: I love my quartz countertops because I never have to seal them. They're beautiful, strong, durable, and exceedingly low-maintenance. I don't have to worry about someone spilling a red glass of wine on them and thinking, *I wish you hadn't done that*. Stain-resistant quartz countertops means I have virtually eliminated that worry.

The bedroom represents another good example of how setting the right foundation for streamlining your belongings makes maintenance so much easier. When you go to a luxe hotel room, there are not a lot of pillows on the bed because housekeepers don't have time to service complex pillow arrangements. Moreover, the clean lines of an uncluttered bed are easier to look at *and* relax into. At home, I make my bed as soon as we're up, not because I am a good person but because I am trying to take care of myself. I can make it expertly and beautifully in less than ninety seconds. Here's how I do it. First, we use a coverlet or a duvet with a comforter instead of a bedspread. Pull up the comforter or coverlet, smooth it flat—and I'm pretty much done.

I don't believe in having a hundred decorative pillows on the bed. Instead, in my bedroom, I have just one large decorative throw pillow on the bed to make a statement. I keep our king-sized sleeping pillows behind king shams (standard shams should go in front of standard sleeping pillows) and in front of Euro shams, which serve as a comfortable, protective barrier between us and the headboard. Though I prefer a single, large decorative pillow on a king-sized bed, these beds can take up to three. With smaller beds (queen, full, and twin), it's best to keep decorative or accent pillows to one statement-making splash of color or texture. You can see it does not take a lot of time to make your bed if you do not make it hard on yourself.

STORE EFFICIENTLY, CURATE CAREFULLY, DISPLAY PROUDLY

The second step—the harder one—after you have established your foundation is maintaining your space so that it always looks and feels its best. This often means changing your habits—not easy, I know, but absolutely doable and totally worth it. The key is figuring out (1) what things you absolutely need to have around to keep your life running smoothly, and (2) what you absolutely *want* to have around because you *love* them ("like" is not enough) for their beauty, sentimental value, or some other intrinsic characteristic that makes the object essential to you. Everything else can—should—go.

Too often, we keep things because we think they could be useful or needed *one day*, only to find that the time never came around. Meanwhile, there's a cost associated with keeping items we don't need: the cost of visual clutter, stuff management and maintenance, and the stress that comes with it. I also think that the things you *do* keep around should have designated spots in storage or on display, like the designated knife drawer in my kitchen. If an object, be it utilitarian or aesthetic, makes the cut to keep around, then it's earned the right to have a place of its own.

Think about it: you come home from work, you're tired, and instead of breathing a sigh of relief when you walk into your home, you are confronted with the chaotic sight of the stuff you were too tired to put away the night before. This stuff has a tendency to build up over time so that eventually it's overwhelming, especially when you don't even know where to put all that stuff. *Where do I put this?* If you can't answer that question, whatever it is ends up not going anywhere, and you feel stressed and defeated. So, I say again: if you need it, you need to find a place to put it.

But even when you find that perfect place, you have to reckon with our all-too-human need to take up space, use it, and fill it. Knowing how to display our objects, and how many of them to display, can be a challenge. Even the most spacious museum doesn't have all of its collection on display at any one time. Instead, it exhibits pieces that together tell a story but that also stand alone, each as a rightful focus of attention. When you are selecting among your things for decoration and display, think like a museum curator. Give each object an opportunity to shine; if you love it, treat it with respect. It will delight you even more.

Remember this wisdom attributed to the great designer Coco Chanel: "Simplicity is the keynote of all true elegance." If you look at a room and think, *Maybe it could use one more thing*, stop right there! Refrain from adding that one last thing. When there is too much stuff to appreciate the craftsmanship of things, you miss out on experiencing the effort and care that went into making the objects in your home. This encapsulates the compromise position I advocate—you don't need to go full minimalist to create and enjoy soothing spaces. Surround yourself with things you love, but give them room to breathe, and remember that less really can be more relaxing!

Your beautiful objects shine even more brightly when you rearrange them or (temporarily) retire them. This requires little to no additional monetary investment, and I end up appreciating these items more when they're presented in an entirely new light. The artworks above my fireplace mantels and headboards, for example, are all about the same size, so rotating them around is easily accomplished without exposing the picture hangers.

After a rotation and refresh, it feels like I've gotten new stuff but without the actual cost and time of acquisition! Additionally, I rotate out throw pillows, throws, and bedding, which is a great way to renew a space while extending the life span of these items by limiting their yearly use and exposure. Keep a log of what you own so you are mindful that you still have it and can change it out. Even when you see something beautiful out of the corner of your eye as you walk from one room to another, you appreciate its presence.

High-end properties invest time and effort into making sure their guests feel pampered. Each time a guest checks into an establishment, the hotelier has only one chance to make that all-important first impression, so it has to be right the first time. Beyond that, it also has to be right the second, third, and fourth time as well—because repeat business depends on it, so these properties maintain a strict routine of maintenance and replenishment. You can do the same thing at home.

Don't forget the small extras that make a huge difference in the look and feel of a home, taking it from being just the practical place where your stuff dwells up to a property that feels like a posh resort. Fresh flowers, fruit in a bowl, a wonderful fragrance wafting through a room are just some of these special elements. You can more easily and economically maintain those special touches with the right choices. It is key to choose fresh flower and fruit options that stay vibrant for weeks (and sometimes months) rather than days; use room fragrances like diffusers that work for months without necessitating an action by you; and make other choices that turn maintenance into extra minutes of your time rather than extra hours.

WINDOW WISDOM

"One of the easiest ways to understand the importance of windows in a well-designed home is to imagine a home without any windows at all. It quickly becomes clear how critical windows and doors are to the home," says Christine Marvin, director of corporate strategy and design at Marvin Windows and Doors, which provides windows and doors for quality properties in a wide array of locales. A number of studies have uncovered the positive impact sunlight and natural air have on productivity and well-being. We know, and we can feel the value of sunlight through a door or fresh air coming through a window. The health benefits have been well documented in other environments, such as health-care facilities, making it easy to see how those benefits can also be realized at home. While you may not be able to replace all your windows and doors, they are an important and often overlooked part of home design, and attention to how they look can have an impact on the vacation feel of all your rooms.

KEEP WINDOWS SPARKLING. It's essential for connecting us with what's outside—sunrises and sunsets, views of nature, views of a city. These are the things that allow us to experience life and allow us to relate to our surroundings. "We often walk into a room and get a gut feeling—'I love this space'—and it's often the way light helps the room to feel airy or cozy or open or private that serves as a significant contributor to that feeling of connectivity to a space," says Christine. Make sure your windows and glass doors are sparkling clean inside and out to take advantage of the light and the views.

ACCENTUATE WINDOWS AND DOORS WITH PLANTS AND GREENERY. "It not only helps my plants thrive but also creates a natural indoor/outdoor connection to the plant life outdoors," says Christine. "Using a neutral color palette that doesn't distract from what's happening outside my walls, I'm able to achieve an uncluttered, soothing interior that feels cohesive. Those spaces are where I can truly unwind and appreciate the surrounding nature."

LARGE WINDOWS AND DOORS CREATE AN IDEAL TRANSITION POINT from indoors to outdoors that, when open, "can leave you wondering if you're still inside or if you've stepped outside in the best way possible," according to Christine. Many homeowners use large doors to create the illusion of more indoor space while gaining greater light, more natural air, and a huge connection to the outdoors. If you can't widen your windows and doors (which requires structural work), consider replacing existing solid doors with glass-paned doors and paned windows with those that are one unobstructed piece of glass.

COORDINATE INDOOR/OUTDOOR SPACES to create a flow between the areas—this helps make windows and glass doors appear larger, too.

ORGANIZATION & CLEANLINESS

The first step toward decluttering your visual landscape and subsequently decluttering your mind is to designate a place for necessary, everyday items to go. The second, and equally important, is getting in the habit of putting things *back* in their designated spots. I believe in this simple rule so strongly that my husband and I have been teaching the kids to follow it. They know to neatly line up their shoes in the mudroom and to put their toys back in their designated spots after playing with them.

Of course, children are naturally exuberant, so it doesn't make sense to let their occasional messes rattle you, but reinforcing the message of respecting our things, keeping them neat, and setting that example by modeling it makes teaching a routine of putting things away a little easier. The end result is worth it—because kids especially, in spite of their boundless energy, also crave order and consistency. Our kids, for example, usually know where a specific toy or piece of clothing is when they want it. There's hardly ever the question of "Dad, do you know where my [insert whatever you like here] is?" In my opinion, a chaotic household can be no better for a child than it is for an adult—it may be even worse.

Immediately putting dirty dishes into the dishwasher post-meal is another good example of forming a habit that reduces clutter and the ensuing stress it creates. I happen to be fanatical about putting things in the dishwasher. Keep in mind that your kitchen is often one of the first spaces that greets you in the morning. Instead of the message being "Hey, you've got gross dishes to still deal with and load," let it be "Good morning! I'm here and ready to go to work!" Like many folks, we have to get two kids up, fed, and dressed for school in the morning, so the last thing I need to contend with is a mess from the night before. Likewise, I don't need to see the aftermath of breakfast sitting around all day in the kitchen sink. The simple truth is, if you deal with the mess when you make it, it stops being a mess right away and you can get on with your day without the burden of disorder lurking in the background. Ignoring it doesn't make it go away! Not attending to small messes quickly often means that the task of cleaning it up gets bigger, harder, and more time consuming to tackle.

It's important to remember that each time you enter a room in your home, it makes an impression on you and others, and it also sends a clear message—positive or negative. The great news is that you have complete control over that message and its contents. To ensure that my home is filled with as many positive messages of calm and relaxation as possible, my family and I have gotten into the habit of quickly resetting each room after we're done using it. By doing this consistently, the amount of time we spend cleaning up and neatening is practically close to zero because rooms don't fall into a state of complete disarray.

Making your bed first thing in the morning and re-fluffing the throw pillows on your couch before you leave the room allow you to enter the next time without having to make the mental note that something is out of place and now on an expanding to-do list. By getting into the habit of resetting a visual landscape each time we use it, it's not only more doable and easier to maintain, we've also helped set a tone that's more relaxing and thus more vacation-like. Of course, most luxury hotels and resorts have a staff that will do the resetting, but for most of us, having hired help to reset on a daily basis just isn't feasible or even desirable. Luckily, it's not necessary. Like going to the gym or flossing your teeth, once you incorporate this low-level maintenance into your daily routine, you no longer even think about it. In fact, out of habit, I reset the

visual in the hotel rooms I stay in so they remain pleasing to look at. Although it certainly helps the housekeeper, I do it primarily for me and my enjoyment of the space.

Have you ever considered how a hotel housekeeper refreshes a room you're occupying over several nights? Professional housekeeping staff are taught skills that make them amazingly efficient and effective; an accomplished housekeeper wipes down surfaces, empties trash receptacles, vacuums, replenishes necessities, put things that you might've moved back in their designated spaces, and makes the bed. If you are a slob, a staffer picks up your stuff and stacks it neatly. All in twenty minutes or less. If they can do it, you can do it, too. It's all about establishing a routine and sticking with it so that little jobs stay little, and you're always caught up with your chores.

Encourage other members of your household to do the same. Closed storage doors, drawers, and boxes help keep you organized. If you *must* have some amount of clutter, see if you can relegate it to one room, preferably with a door, so clutter is confined to just one area and not spread throughout your home. This allows you the chance to chip away at these possibly extraneous items in one place instead of having each room in your home in less-than-optimal condition. At least temporarily, think of that room as the "back of house" of a hotel—the place where administrative duties are carried out, away from guests' view. It's not meant to be seen at that moment but still should be addressed to function properly. Even if you live in a studio or one bedroom, keep the clutter in one place, whether it's a designated cabinet in the kitchen or within a piece of furniture with storage, so the rest of your place is pleasant and enjoyable to be in while you tackle your one dysfunctional area.

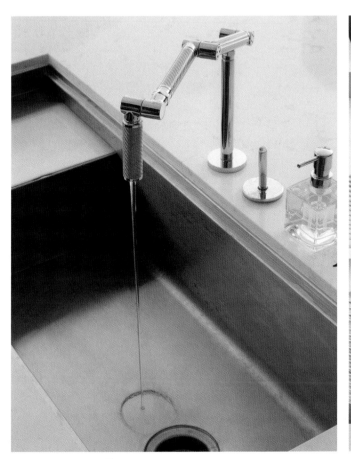

FURRY MESSES:
CLEANING UP AFTER FAMILY PETS

Our family includes four big dogs that we adore, so we have the extra challenge of dealing with the inevitable dog hair that gets shed no matter what and dealing with their physical needs. In fact, the total weight of dog in our home exceeds that of the total human weight! If you have pets, you, too, likely know how much they bring to your life and how they become cherished parts of your family. And you also realize that keeping your pet-friendly home looking great requires thought and effort! Here's what I do to maintain a tidy dog-friendly home with minimal effort. This routine works for our family, but you should, of course, determine what works for yours.

Our dogs have free rein of specific areas where our family spends our most waking hours, such as the kitchen, family room, living room, breakfast room, and our home offices. We've taught them that our bedrooms are off limits. Instead, they've been given their own room in the house, where they each have a bed and where they take their meals. Similarly, we sectioned off a part of our yard that's primarily for humans so that the kids have a place to play without fear of stepping in something undesirable. The dogs come out to play with the family in this restricted space, too, but it's not where they go to do their daily business. Instead, we have a *hardscaped* space, peppered with smaller soft areas covered with bark mulch, where they can poop and pee, so that even in bad weather, they don't bring muddy paw prints with them when they come back inside.

We keep towels in the mudroom to dry them off after they've been out in the rain, so that "wet dog" odor doesn't permeate the house. Likewise, their leashes, collars, and toys are stored neatly in the mudroom. I realize not everyone will have the room, inside or out, to create specific areas designated for pets, but the idea here is to contain the areas that you will need to maintain. Even if you only designate the single most difficult area to maintain as off limits to your pets (like a formal sitting room or playroom), you've saved yourself work and made your home that much easier to take care of.

That leaves dealing with the dog hair. All—and I mean *all*—of our upholstery in rooms where the dogs are allowed is performance fabric or indoor/outdoor fabric; this makes it easier to keep these spaces neat and clean. For those of you who aren't familiar with the term *performance fabrics*, they are primarily indoor fabrics that have been designed and manufactured to be stain-resistant and permanently cleanable. They've been tested with an array of stains, including those from makeup, wine, chocolate, and a broad assortment of food. Using them allows your upholstered sofas and chairs to accommodate kids eating ice cream and dogs taking naps. It doesn't mean we don't have to pull fur off our surfaces, but it does mean we never have to put a towel on the sofa or the carpet. On furniture pieces where I don't have performance fabrics or indoor/outdoor fabrics, I employ spray-on coatings that treat fabric to make it more stain- and even UV ray–resistant. Vacuuming is done by both me and my powerful Dyson and a robot vacuum, and both are done daily.

There are breeds, such as the Portuguese water dog or labradoodle, that do not shed—so there are alternative breeds of dogs for animal lovers who simply cannot vacuum every day. Making smart choices in advance is a key part of building the foundation that's best going to support you, your family, and your lifestyle. Since our family is committed to dog adoption, no matter the breed, we've simply built their care and cleanup into our household routine, which is the advice that I impart to you. For pet lovers, the reward of their affection makes the upkeep involved worth it.

BEFORE YOU CHECK OUT . . .

• Schedule routine household maintenance.

» **VACUUMING:** I know that I'm likely in the minority, but I love to vacuum. For me, it's a stress reducer that provides immediate satisfaction. Although I vacuum at least twice a day (I live with about five hundred pounds of dog, after all), the general rule of thumb is that you should be vacuuming once a week for each person, cat, and dog (other furry family members actively using floor space count, too) in the house. For our family, that translates to four humans and four dogs, necessitating a minimum of eight vacuuming sessions a week.

» **CLOTHING:** Try not to leave clothing on the floor. I put away clothing items that can be re-worn each night before I go to bed rather than having to wake up to it strewn on the floor or on furniture. Unless they're dirty, sweaters and jeans get folded and shirts get hung. Items that need to get laundered, like socks, go straight into the laundry hamper. It's easier for me to do at night because my mornings are hectic with getting the kids off to school and getting myself ready for the start of the workday.

» **SHEETS AND TOWELS:** Wash every four to five days if used daily. I'm often on the road, sleeping in hotels several nights a week, but I still keep track of how many nights my sheets have been slept on. If possible, I make my bed with freshly laundered and ironed sheets before I go out of town to ensure that I receive the softest landing possible when I return home. It's not dissimilar to walking into a neat and clean hotel room!

PART 2

EVERYDAY VACATION HOME ROOM BY ROOM

Now that I have laid out the basics of designing and keeping your home "vacation ready," it's time to drill down more deeply into the details that make each room in your house a relaxing and carefree space. In the next three chapters, I share what I think are the best choices to make the unique qualities of living and family rooms, dining spaces, kitchens and baths, bedrooms, and even utility and tech rooms as welcoming and peaceful as possible.

CHAPTER 3
LIVING AND DINING

If you look at just about any top-ten list of what makes us happy, you'll find that the top spot is usually reserved for relationships with supportive family and friends. And home is where you spend the most time with the people who matter most to you. The joy of making your home feel like a retreat means creating an environment that is also conducive to easy-going, meaningful interactions with your loved ones and guests.

In this chapter, we look at all the touchpoints that create welcoming spaces: the entryway, which sets the tone for you and your family and visitors as they come into the house; common areas like family and living rooms where people sit and talk or enjoy entertainment; and the dining room, where we share meals or even a quiet cup of tea that helps us regroup on our own or that facilitates intimate or lively conversations. I also include the great outdoors, as patios, porches, and gardens have become an important part of the restorative nature of the vacation experience at home.

FOYERS AND MUDROOMS

Every home, no matter how big or small, should greet you warmly the minute you enter it. Hotels use foyers and entrances as a key tool to impress their visitors, get them to relax the moment they walk in, and make them feel they are someone and somewhere special. Re-create that wonderful hotel greeting by implementing a foyer design that acknowledges you warmly when you enter. Place a mirror and a console table with drawers—a tiny table with a drawer or even a wall-mounted ledge will do just fine in a small space—in the entry point to serve as a designated spot for incoming mail, magazines, catalogs, keys, and dog leashes. Having these everyday items accessible but out of sight decreases the visual clutter while keeping your entryway super functional.

No matter the size of your home, the same is true. Its foyer, or entrance way, introduces you, your family, and guests to the retreat that lies within. This area sets the tone for the rest of your house. It's the first-impression space where you and your family are first greeted, so make it beautiful, dynamic, and easy to keep clean.

Keeping shoes and coats out of sight creates a more relaxing atmosphere upon entering your home. Put these items away in coat closets, in a nearby pantry, or in your bedroom closet. In my tiny New York apartment, where no mudroom or pantry exists, I've designated a small space inside a nearby kitchen base cabinet for frequently worn shoes for that season.

More and more homes feature a mudroom, which, as its name implies, is not the front-of-house entrance that the foyer is. A mudroom is the casual side entrance to the home that's often—but not always—off the kitchen. Don't fall into the trap of confusing "casual" with "messy." *Do*

think about how your family uses the space; my family is run as many traditional Asian households are, so we take off our shoes when we come in the door. We line them up in the mudroom so that, once again, the unaesthetic clutter of running shoes, kids' sneakers, and loafers is stored away and out of sight. A mudroom is also the perfect spot for keeping the dogs' gear (leashes, Frisbees, etc.), umbrellas, backpacks, and other bulky items that you use daily. Keep these tips in mind:

- Make your mudroom as storage friendly as possible; figure out how much space you think you'll need, then enlarge that by 10–15 percent. The more people who live in your house, the more storage you need. Consider what each person in your household likes to do. For instance, kids who play lacrosse may need more space than those who play basketball because of the differences in required equipment. Avid bike riders may need more room than runners. Large families probably buy more food than smaller households, so if that is your situation, create a large pantry and build in enough space to discreetly stow more reusable shopping bags near the door you use most frequently. Keep these final tips in mind:

  » If space and budget permit, add a sink and a vanity to your mudroom. That way, the grit and grime from the great outdoors never even make it into the main part of your home.

  » Be sure your window treatments are not the type that reach the floor. Keep foyers and mudrooms neat by opting for wooden or Roman blinds.

FORMAL AND INFORMAL ROOMS

While the multipurpose—or *great*—room craze shows no signs of abating, formal living rooms often remain an important part of both old and new builds. As the names of these rooms imply, they are the areas of the home where we live—whether it be to entertain and impress (*yes!*) important guests, or to spend time with the most important people in our lives—family and friends. Even though the styles we use to decorate these rooms may differ, the principles of tranquility and simplicity we use to guide their design remain largely the same.

Keep in mind one core principle as you furnish your living and multipurpose rooms: Purchase wisely and choose furnishings that require minimal maintenance.

Again, the more you build ease of care and low maintenance into your design and decor, the less effort you expend keeping your spaces looking their best. Unlike a hotel, there's likely not a staff of people in your home helping with upkeep.

So, as you plan your living or multipurpose room, think about furnishing it with pieces that require minimal maintenance. For beauty, function, and low-maintenance durability, consider the following:

- Tight-back upholstery (as opposed to sofas and chairs that have loose or removable pillow backs) minimizes the amount of fluffing and fussing you will have to do every time someone sits on a couch or a chair. The tight back can be just as comfortable and supplemented with throw pillows for a softer back if desired.

- Reversible seat cushions save you time and energy by doubling the useful life of the cushion.

- Performance fabrics and indoor/outdoor fabrics help reduce the time and effort you must devote to keeping upholstered furniture clean and fresh. The performance fabrics I use are made to resist stains and are permanently cleanable for the foreseeable life of the furniture. They are ideal for heavily used areas and everyday family use. Many of these fabrics are factory treated to ensure their durability. Another durable alternative is leather, although too much of it in any one room can be overpowering. Coating and treating your fabrics after the fact can also help keep them stain-resistant—though, unlike performance and indoor/outdoor fabrics, these coatings will eventually need to be reapplied to keep their protective properties in play.

- Maintenance-free tabletops eliminate the need for placemats, coasters, and other protective contrivances—really, just clutter—as well as your stress-inducing, nervous hypervigilance that comes from watching and waiting for your kids to spill something or a guest to drop his wineglass:

  » Quartz, slate, and glass tops are easy options since wine, salsa, ketchup, and other materials that can leave stains can't penetrate and stain these surfaces.

  » Glass tops made specifically to place over your treasured wooden furniture pieces can be an easy and relatively inexpensive way to keep them from stains and scratches.

  » Durable wood surfaces are good options, too. Teak, mahogany, ipe, redwood, and other wood species that can withstand exterior elements are, of course, usable indoors as well as outdoors. Additionally, a handful of furniture artisans, like Clay Aronson of Aronson Woodworks, are crafting solid-wood furniture with highly-durable finishes that allow the wood surface to resist stains, moisture, and scratches without the protection of a glass top. Perfect for families and people who entertain frequently!

- Limit wood tones to create a feeling of calm. This doesn't mean that all the wood tones in a single space must match; rather, it means that having the wood tones within a single room relate to one another through shared undertones can eliminate one more unique element your eye picks up. For example, as long as the general tone of wood is the same, and the style of furniture is compatible, mixing teak and walnut and even oak pieces together is fine. Rather than stimulating your eye, a common color scheme in wood pieces helps soothe the eye and creates a calming, quiet atmosphere.

- Stain-resistant carpeting has come a long way in the past few years, evolving into a thing of beauty as well as a durable performer. I love performance (6,6) nylon for both rugs and carpeting because I've found it to be great for pets and kids due to its antimicrobial, stain-resistant, and fade-resistant properties. It is also soft underfoot and comes in a wide variety of colors. At this stage of my life, with a young family and four big dogs, this is one of the best choices for me in high-traffic areas.

DINING ROOMS

Dining rooms are wonderful spaces that help us create memories by acting as the stage for holiday meals and other important gatherings. Unfortunately, I have seen dining rooms turn into dumping grounds for school paraphernalia, mail and other paperwork, and even laundry! Why not give this room the respect it deserves by keeping clutter out and employing these simple strategies for keeping it celebration-worthy and soothing to the eye?

- Closed storage—either built-in cabinetry or a china cabinet with solid doors—can stow most dishes and silverware. Divided drawers are especially helpful to keep flatware and serving utensils organized and at the ready.

- Open shelving should be reserved for displaying special serving pieces in a dining area. These unique pieces, like large compotes and bowls or soup tureens, do double duty as artwork when not needed for a meal.

- Rugs under dining tables should extend far enough out so that when chairs are pulled out the legs of the chairs stay on the rugs.

- Keep centerpieces simple; a sculptural, decorative piece can be interesting on its own. Larger-scaled bowls of apples or a large vase of simple green leaves adds drama, color, and texture without fuss or a lot of effort. Covering the top of a bowl with dry sheet moss is also a great way to add a low-maintenance organic component to your table. This can be easily accomplished by creating a foundation with florist foam, Styrofoam peanuts, or even crumpled-up newspaper. The dried moss can then be laid on top and misted every week or so. Though it will eventually lose its vibrant color, dried moss makes a no-fuss display for at least several months. And all these alternatives often last much longer, and require less upkeep, than many fresh-cut flowers (see my list of long-lasting cut flowers on page 21).

OUTDOOR LIVING

Comfortable, inviting outdoor spaces can be the most magical of all spaces. Whether your home's outdoor space is a tiny balcony or a sprawling front and back lawn, you can evoke the luxurious at-one-with-nature feel of a vacation retreat. Resort landscaping caters to the specific desires of the guests, whether they are couples seeking a private oasis or business travelers in need of a respite from the demands of meetings and conferences, or families seeking a place for fun.

Apply this same goal to your outside space by asking yourself what you want and need from the space: A place for kids and dogs to run around? Space for hosting large gatherings or intimate entertaining? Do you like to putter in the garden? Or do you just want a space to relax and enjoy a cup of coffee in the morning, or a glass of wine in the evening? Design the space to work for your needs so that you don't expend time and effort later fighting with the original design because it doesn't work for how you want to use it.

No matter what the intended purpose of your outdoor space, there are certain universal principles to keep in mind:

• Orient furniture toward the view and away from unattractive sights like fences, walls, or storage areas.

• Avoid, if you can, sight lines into interior spaces—especially those of your neighbors!

• Have a mix of sunny and shady areas.

• Avoid blocking views from your interior spaces with plants and outdoor furnishings.

Many resorts and retreats have moved away from highly stylized gardens to a more natural landscape that takes advantage of local flora and is kinder to the environment—and oftentimes these gardens require less maintenance. Even though resorts have large maintenance staffs to mow lawns, water grass, rake leaves, and sweep away debris on a daily basis, they also want to minimize the amount of care their gardens require. To that end, they often employ hardscaping, artificial turf, evergreens, succulents, and container gardening (large decorative pots) to allow for efficient maintenance.

Applying these hotel trends to your own space, ask yourself if you can replace fussy perennial beds with indigenous grasses and easy-care shrubs. Or use more native plants in general, thus eliminating the need to water frequently, add amendments to the soil, and fret about weather conditions overall—*because you have selected plants that will thrive "as is" in that location.*

Also look for plants that don't shed leaves so you don't have to do a lot of cleanup throughout the year. Plants that don't have dramatic life cycles, like pine trees and many shrubs, and that stay green year-round are easy to maintain and provide something green to look at during winter months. When choosing trees, you can select species that only drop their leaves or needles once a year, which lessens the time you have to spend raking up after them.

There's so much more that could be written about landscaping and gardening. So much useful advice, however, depends on the size and shape of your outdoor space, the growing zone where you live, the amount of time you want to dedicate to your yard, and your personal taste. There are some general principles, though, that work for me and that I use when designing outdoor space for myself and my clients to deliver maximum, positive visual impact with minimal maintenance.

Keep your options open. An expansive green lawn is a thing of beauty, but it's also not the right choice for many of us. We may not have the space required for a large, lush lawn; we may not want (or be permitted by local ordinances) to use the hundreds of gallons of water it takes to keep a lawn looking green; we may not want to spend the time (or money) it takes to keep the lawn properly trimmed; or we just want another look for our outdoor space. There are alternatives:

- **Artificial turf.** Forget about the hideous neon-green plastic "grass" that was the early version of artificial turf. Today's turf is gorgeous. In my opinion, it also feels good underfoot, is pet-friendly, and is virtually maintenance-free. I am a fan of using it in smaller spaces where you want a bit of green, especially in those areas that are shady, or where the soil needs a lot of amending to support a lawn. An added benefit is that artificial turf does not require watering, making it potentially more environmentally friendly.

- **Ground-covering plants.** Don't limit your imagination to just grass. There are many plants that spread quickly and provide attractive ground cover with color and texture. If you have a space that is hard to mow or is in a very shady spot, or if you are looking for a contrasting element, think about plants such as pachysandra. Pachysandra works in growing zones four through seven and is dense, leafy, and rapidly spreading. It has tiny white flowers in the spring. When first planted, pachysandra requires frequent watering, but, once established, it is very low maintenance. Other options include clover, thyme (which smells terrific), mazus, and creeping Jennie. Spreading plants vary in their maintenance needs—mostly trimming to keep them out of areas where they're not welcome—but none of them requires the work of a traditional grass lawn.

- **Hardscaping.** If you have a smallish plot of land for outdoor living, you might want to consider a patio. There are many possibilities for creating attractive low-maintenance patios, from budget-friendly pavers to timeless but extravagant slate or bluestone. Patios, walkways, rock gardens, and low stone walls can please the eye and turn your outdoors into a highly functional living area.

- **Water features and pools.** The sound and sight of water can often bring a sense of calm and relaxation to a home. Whether it's a pool or a major fountain, a water element of some sort is usually found at most luxury hotels and resorts for this very reason. Beautiful to look at when done correctly, swimming pools create a serene environment that can soothe the most restless spirit—though *serene* is probably not the right adjective when the kids are splashing around with their friends at a pool party! It's true that pools require frequent maintenance, but if you choose carefully, you can reduce some of those chores. Fiberglass pools, for instance, are virtually leakproof, unlike gunite, which periodically requires patching, or vinyl, which periodically needs a replacement liner. If you build a pool cover into your budget, moreover, you can reduce the amount of skimming and filter-cleaning you will need to do.

- **Evergreens.** Over the last few years, I have been making greater and greater use of evergreens in my landscapes. First of all, I appreciate their all-season beauty. Evergreens always give color to a garden even in the dead of winter. Many, like yew and holly, offer colorful berries for at least part of the year. Best of all, there is a wide choice. Broadleaf boxwood and holly look great up against the house to camouflage dreary foundation walls. They also make good borders and can help define private spaces within the yard. All variety of spruce are also no-shedders, dropping their needles only every two years or so.

- **Containers.** Large planters define spaces such as an outdoor dining area and bring greenery to balconies, terraces, and patios with containers. One to three large containers make a more soothing yet dramatic appearance than dozens of little pots scattered about the area. Additionally, larger containers will expand your choices by accommodating a greater range of plant sizes and types. Containers are ideal for just about every kind of plant—from annuals that will brighten their area for just one season to boxwoods, which stay green year-round and require little more than an occasional pruning. In addition, boxwoods do not shed their leaves!

If you live in a cold-weather climate that's prone to freezes, select containers made out of galvanized steel, zinc, wood, fiberglass, or with frames wrapped in synthetic rattan or resin wicker. These materials remain largely unaffected by freeze-and-thaw cycles that wreak havoc on terra-cotta or concrete pots that can absorb water and freeze, expand, and fracture the pot. If you love pots made of these materials, bring them in before the first frost, and make sure they are thoroughly dry and empty. Alternatively, you can cover them to seal out rain and snow; this is an unsightly solution, however, that leaves you spending the winter months looking at empty pots swaddled in plastic sheeting.

FIND YOUR GARDENING SWEET SPOT

The USDA Plant Hardiness Zone Map, which you can find easily online, is an indispensable tool for finding the trees, shrubs, plants, and flowers that will thrive in your region. Knowing your zone and subzone will save you the disappointment of planting something that will not do well or, worse yet, die.

Each zone has a wide variety of plants that require minimal maintenance. Unless you are a dedicated gardener or enjoy this as a hobby, these are the plantings you should use in your flower beds, borders, and accent areas for your best chance of success. When you plant flowers, think perennials; you plant them once, and they bloom year after year. This is about as low maintenance as you can get! Examples that do well in multiple zones include daylilies that produce gorgeous blossoms and sturdy greenery that lasts even after the blossoms fade; hosta, which features broad leaves in a variety of colors and long-stemmed blooms; and spirea, a compact shrub that produces delicate blooms and is very forgiving of both neglect and zealous pruning.

Seek out advice at your local garden center—it's usually free and it's based on knowledge of your local conditions. Many garden centers also offer a replacement guarantee, either for a limited time or for the life of your plant, so changing out a dead plant doesn't have to become a financial stressor. Just make sure that you digitize those receipts or organize them in a physical file.

Questions to ask when you are trying to figure out what plants to buy include:

- Do I love to garden and have time for it?

- How often do I water?

- When do I prune? How much do I prune?

- What kind of fertilizer and how often do I apply it?

EXTERIOR FURNITURE CHOICES FOR TIDY, LIVABLE, AND EASY-TO-MAINTAIN SPACES

We talk a lot about "bringing the outdoors in," but when you are designing a deck, patio, or other outdoor seating space, the opposite applies. When you select furniture for your patio, you want to keep in mind many of the same principles of proportion and design we use for indoor furniture, but there are other considerations as well. Here is an overview:

• Choose the right frame for your furniture.

Today's outdoor furniture comes in a wide array of choices, and while your personal preference should play the key role in your selection, some materials do better in some settings than others.

» **Resin wicker.** If the furniture is placed near the pool or other water feature, or if it will be exposed to a lot of rain, think about furniture frames wrapped in resin wicker, a woven synthetic material (polyethylene) designed to resist the elements. Resin wicker is fairly low maintenance as well—it washes off beautifully with a hose.

» **Teak is another great alternative.** It's a weather-resistant hardwood due to its high oil content. Teak is beautiful and very long-lasting but can require consistent maintenance and upkeep if you want to preserve its honey hue, and it can be fairly expensive. If you go with teak, think of your purchase as a long-term investment.

» **Wrought iron** is a smart choice if your property is subject to frequent winds—even in a very stiff breeze, it's likely not going anywhere, and you don't have the worry of your furniture sailing off into the next county. It also often has a custom, handcrafted look that is part of its appeal.

Look for pieces that are powder-coated to prevent rusting, and if you spot rust on your wrought iron

furniture, attend to it immediately by scrubbing it off with a wire brush and treating it with an application of an antirust substance like a specially formulated spray paint or marine varnish.

» **Anodized aluminum can be sleek, stylish, and modern-looking.** Not as heavy as wrought iron, anodized aluminum is nevertheless very durable, though not great near salt water due to the possibility of corrosion. Keep in mind that many anodized aluminum frames require special maintenance products specified by the manufacturers to keep their warranties valid.

• Choose the right foam and textiles for your cushions.

Just as you want to find the perfect frame for your outdoor furniture, you want to make sure you've got the best foam and fabric for your seat cushions. All outdoor cushions should have cores made from quick-drying foam specifically manufactured to endure the elements, especially water. This is key if you are handy and plan to make your own cushions or if you are having cushions custom made. Look for anti-mildew upholstery foam for outdoor and marine furniture. The ideal fabric cushions for outdoor furniture are not delicate; they need to be made out of comfortable but durable materials that can stand up to the elements, casual entertaining, and dripping-wet guests plunking down after a swim. Cushion fabric has to look and feel good, work hard, and be easy to maintain! That's asking a lot of any fabric, but fortunately there are many choices that fit the bill:

» **Solution-dyed polypropylene (olefin) with high-energy dyed polyester (Inside Out Performance fabrics):** Perhaps at the forefront of indoor/outdoor fabric technology, this combination is highly durable, water-resistant, mold- and mildew-resistant, fade-resistant, more affordable, bleach cleanable, and with the big

advantage of accommodating a wider range of designs that meet today's demand for beautiful, soft fabrics that perform inside or outside the home. These fabrics also uniquely utilize a bio-based, PFC-free liquid repellant that is more environmentally friendly. Unlike solution-dyed acrylics, these fabrics will not easily pill.

» **Solution-dyed acrylics:** Because these yarns are dyed as the yarn is being extruded, fabrics with this fabrication are noted for high levels of color saturation and light fastness, which means that they are among the most resistant to fading. And, like other indoor/outdoor fabrics, solution-dyed acrylics are water-resistant, bleach cleanable, and mold- and mildew-resistant. They are, unfortunately, noted for a tendency to pill and are generally more costly due to a higher cost of manufacturing.

» **Solution-dyed polypropylene (olefin):** Fabrics in this category offer superior durability (no pilling) and are water-resistant, fade-resistant, mold- and mildew-resistant, and bleach cleanable. Solution-dyed polypropylene also tends to have a more approachable price point than solution-dyed acrylics though oil-based stains can be difficult to clean and these fabrics can become brittle from too much sunlight exposure if UV inhibitors are not employed.

» **Solution-dyed polyester:** Indoor/outdoor fabrics in this category will be about the same price point as solution-dyed polypropylene and solution-dyed polypropylene with high-energy polyester options (and generally less expensive than solution-dyed acrylic options) but may have less light fastness, which means they may fade sooner. Solution-dyed polyester options will still exhibit resistance to mold, mildew, and water and will be bleach cleanable.

• Choose the right rugs and accessories.

Adding a rug to an outdoor space can be a nice grounding force but also a lot of work, especially if your rug isn't sitting under some kind of roof. Outdoor rugs just add one more thing to keep neat and clean and can, therefore, be stress-inducing rather than a relaxing element. If you feel differently, however, look for indoor-outdoor rugs made of olefin for durability, comfort, color, and ease of maintenance. Natural fibers such as sisal require constant maintenance and, many think, are not as comfortable under bare feet as synthetics such as olefin. They'll also disintegrate more quickly, especially if completely exposed to the elements.

Similarly, accessories in your outdoor seating area can be kept minimal and simple. Go for fewer but bigger statement pieces like planters, decorative bowls, and candleholders in easy-to-maintain materials, such as concrete, ceramic, teak, stainless steel, and anodized aluminum. Flameless pillar candles provide warmth and soft light during the evening, and they don't extinguish in the breeze. If you prefer real candles, I highly recommend using hurricane-style lanterns and candleholders with protective glass covers so that the flame stands a better chance of staying lit.

Indoors or out, the public spaces of your home should delight your family and your guests. They should reveal something about your personality and provide the setting for the things you treasure and want others to enjoy and admire. For example, my spaces express a love of fine art photography, world travel, and clean lines. But these public spaces should also delight *you* and invite you to spend time in them—time you enjoy, not time spent exerting endless effort to keep them looking their best.

BEFORE YOU CHECK OUT . . .

- Every home should greet you warmly and impressively when you enter it. Remember that you and your family are your home's most important people.

- First impressions count. Make sure the entrances to your home are clutter-free and that you have adequate storage for the things that would otherwise intrude on the serenity of this all-important space.

- Have a place for everything; don't allow "things" to run your life. If it's beautiful to look at and brings you joy, display it with respect; if it's essential to your daily life, find a convenient place to store it.

- Think before you buy. Acquire and keep only the things you need or treasure the most.

- Think AGAIN before you buy. Consider the costs of maintenance, in terms of time and money, when making a purchase of furnishings. Look for materials that are durable and easy to keep looking good.

CHAPTER 4

SLEEPING AND BATHING

Even the busiest households need private spaces that are truly personal havens. The bedroom and the bathroom fit naturally into this category, as they are the spaces where we turn for replenishment and a moment of calm. You should be able to genuinely rest and rejuvenate in your bedroom, while the bathroom is a place to get your day started from a fresh perspective or to wash away the cares of the day in the evening.

In this chapter, we see how you can not only design these spaces to be relaxing and soothing—but how to keep them that way. Because bed and bath are considered personal spaces in a home, we can sometimes take them for granted, and make them less of a priority in terms of keeping them neat and orderly compared to public spaces. My philosophy is that personal spaces are the most important to keep beautiful, clutter-free, and soothing. I have found ways to minimize the work and time involved in keeping personal spaces maintained, and I share those secrets here with you. After all, when people tell me they want their bedroom and bath to look like a "hotel room" what they are really saying is that they want these rooms to be serene, clean, and clutter-free.

BEDROOMS

Picture your ideal luxury hotel bedroom. It's probably clean, calm, and orderly. It's probably also divided into zones, isn't it? There's the bed for sleeping (and romance!) of course, but there's also a lounge area for reading, watching television, quiet study, or introspection. There's also a mirrored area near the closet for dressing and grooming. There may be a desk for writing letters. You can replicate the calmness of this environment in your bedroom, regardless of its size, even if incorporating all the function isn't doable.

The first step is to decide which activities you want to perform and plan space accordingly. If sleeping isn't the first activity of the plan that springs to mind—uh-oh, back up! You're in the wrong room!

THE BED

Of all the furniture that you own, or will ever own, the bed and its mattress, box spring, and accessories should be among the highest-quality pieces you will ever invest in. We spend one-third of our lives asleep, so it stands to reason that we should make sure this is time well spent—that our sleep is restful and that we don't wake up moaning and groaning thanks to an uncomfortable mattress, a lumpy pillow, or scratchy sheets. These elements need to be tailored to you and your sleeping partner, so spend the time to figure out what components will give you the best night's rest.

Some of the nicest vacation properties offer a pillow menu that allows guests to customize their sleeping experience for maximum relaxation. Why do they do that? Because they understand that a good night's rest is key to being in a relaxed, vacation frame of mind. Each of us sleeps best in a slightly different manner, so getting your bedding components right for you is a critical part of having that vacation experience right at home.

- **Mattress.** Buy the best bed you can afford, and be sure to try before you buy. Check for a good warranty, and research the workmanship of your mattress. This will be the best investment you have ever made for your comfort and your peace of mind. Whether it's spring, memory foam, sponge, or some other construction, plan on replacing the mattress on an eight- to ten-year cycle.

- **Headboards.** Consider a headboard upholstered in a performance fabric (discussed on pages 67 and 69) for ease of maintenance and extra comfort if you tend to sit up in bed to read, watch television, or engage with your laptop.

- **Pillows.** Pillows can be all down (the softest part of a bird—its underbelly—so it's super soft!), or a feather and down combo, all feather, hypoallergenic, memory foam, or some other construction depending on your personal preference. My preference is for a feather-and-down combo pillow—it's not as squashy as an all-down pillow. I also like gusseted pillows, often suggested for side sleepers, which have a side insert of material that allows more of the filling to be more flexible. The pillow that offers you your best possible sleep could be completely different, so take the time to figure out what works best

for you. No matter what you select, pillows that provide consistent, nightly use should be replaced every one to two years. Also, employ pillow protectors to keep pillows looking and smelling as clean as possible. These cotton covers with a zipper on one end are much easier to pop into the washing machine and less expensive than sending your entire pillow out to be laundered.

- **Top of bed—comforter, duvet with comforter insert, coverlet, blanket:** Replace your feather, feather/down combination, or down comforter every fifteen to twenty years. Many may last even longer if properly cared for. Hypoallergenic comforters, stuffed with rayon or synthetic materials, may lose their fluffiness sooner than a down comforter will, but they're also less expensive. Professionally dry-clean your comforter once a year if it's inside a duvet cover; professionally dry-clean it monthly if it's not protected by a duvet (see page 81). Never throw a feather or down comforter into the washing machine. If you do, it'll lose much of its heat-holding capacity. If you'd rather have the option of throwing your comforter in the washing machine, then choose a hypoallergenic comforter, with its more forgiving rayon or synthetic stuffing. Make sure, however, to always check the care instructions before deciding to wash anything yourself.

- **Good-quality sheets** tend to be softer and become more so with regular laundering. They can also last several years if rotated seasonally (for instance, you may want to use your heavier sateen sheets in fall and winter and cooler percale sheets in spring and summer).

For the ultimate luxe, look beyond thread count. For true luxury sleep, 100 percent long-staple cotton is best according to Filippo Arnaboldi, CEO of luxury linen maker Frette. He says consider instead the three Fs of fine sheets: *fiber, finish,* and *feel.* The longer the fiber, the smoother the thread and the softer and more luxurious the sheet, no matter the thread count. Look for sheets marked as long or extra-long cotton fibers for the smoothest feel. The finish means the details that give a sheet a certain look. For example, delicate lace and embroidery give a feminine look, and a plain hem stitch offers a modern touch. As for feel, a sateen weave has the silky-soft feel that caresses the skin, while percale has crisp structure that feels cooler.

In my opinion, white sheets look the most luxurious and inviting. They also help convey cleanliness, which is why hotels and resorts nearly always employ them. When all your sheets are one color, you never have to worry about keeping sets sorted. Replace your sheets every two years if you sleep on them on a nearly daily basis.

Launder every four to five consecutive days of use, then iron your pillowcases and the top and side edges of your flat sheet. This may seem like a big chore, but I've incorporated it into my routine and find that it makes a huge difference in the way my bed looks and my comfort sleeping in it. I personally prefer nice, 100 percent cotton sheets that I pull out of the dryer still slightly damp to reduce the need for intense ironing. Until they're laundered again, having standard shams (or king shams if you have a king bed) and your duvet with comforter or coverlet be the "face" of your made-up bed disguises the wrinkles in between. Of course, there are also plenty of wrinkle-free options, such as microfiber, bamboo, and cotton/polyester blends, that take the ironing out of the process, but—for me, at least—a high-quality cotton sheet is what I sleep best on.

KNOW YOUR BEDDING TERMINOLOGY

There was a time when you'd walk into your hotel room and the first thing you'd see was a heavy and boldly patterned bedspread or comforter. About a decade ago, high-end properties decided to do something different, and they jettisoned the spreads in favor of duvet covers with comforters inside, coverlets, or some combination of the two. The duvet cover with comforter and/or the coverlet continue to reign supreme in hotel rooms, and for good reason: it's an extremely inviting look, simplicity without the forbidding stodginess of a severely tailored bedspread, and much easier to clean and maintain.

Still, there are options you might want to explore when choosing how to dress your bed.

- BLANKET: The simplest of all bed coverings, a blanket's main purpose is to keep you warm. Using a blanket as the bed's covering is minimalist, and, therefore a good option if you are striving for a very pared-down look in your bedroom or live in a relatively warm climate.

- COMFORTER: This is a covering that's filled with down, feathers, or "down alternative" (i.e., a man-made material that mimics the warmth and coziness of down or feathers) without the risk of allergic reactions to those components. Comforters made to go inside a duvet are especially good choices in cool climates. A 100 percent down comforter will be the lightest-weight choice, and the luxury it provides will be priced accordingly. When you are buying a comforter, make sure to check out its warmth level, which will tell you the best choice for your temperature conditions. Comforters that are meant to be the finished, top-of-bed product aren't great choices from a laundering perspective. Not only can they look dated, but they can be bulky and difficult to put in a standard-size washing machine.

- DUVET: This is a fitted cover that encases your comforter. Duvets do double duty—they provide warmth, and they're easy to remove for laundering. For this reason, you'd be hard-pressed to find a comforter without an accompanying duvet employed in even mid-level hotels. Although aesthetics are critical, the cleanliness of bedding is of paramount importance to most guests checking into a property. Unprotected comforters are difficult to launder, yet an easily removable duvet will launder as easily as a flat sheet.

- COVERLETS AND QUILTS: These function as bedspreads; they are two pieces of material sewn together with a filling called *batting* in between. The thicker the coverlet or quilt, the more warmth it provides.

- BEDSPREAD: This is a heavy decorative covering that often needs to be turned back at night for sleeping because of its weight. Bedspreads are dated in appearance and not a popular look these days, but they remain available in a variety of fabrics, from sateen to chenille.

- BED RUNNERS: Splurge on them! There is something special about the luxury this narrow piece of fabric (about twenty-four inches wide and about twenty-four inches longer than the width of your bed size) adds to the end of your bed. It's an easy way to add color to the room and the bed and takes no time at all to neatly place. Throws and blankets are nice, too, but a bed runner is an opportunity to have something really simple and elegant at the end of your bed that doesn't have to be washed on a regular basis. Go for a luxurious material like a silk or something with special details like trim or embroidery. This isn't something that you'll actually sleep with or on . . . so the possibilities of what you can do really can expand. It can add texture and color to the bed, too, without going overboard on a colorful duvet.

SHEET SMARTS

Although I prefer the luxurious feel of pure, extra-long staple, 100 percent Egyptian cotton sheets and am also willing to build into my routine the ironing of my top sheets and pillowcases, you might not be. Here is a quick lesson in the different sheeting options available. Keep in mind that different seasons might call for different kinds of sheets.

- **Cottons:** The most common fiber for bedsheets is *cotton*, with three main varieties: American upland, pima/Supima, and Egyptian. Sea island cotton can also sometimes be found in luxury sheets, though it is extremely expensive to grow and process and is, therefore, in very limited supply. American upland is the most common type of cotton used for sheets and can be either short- or long-staple, which refers to the length of the individual fibers.

  If the label on a sheet or sheet set says "100 percent cotton," it is very likely made from American upland. Sheets made from American upland cotton tend to be more basic in quality (though you can find sheets labeled as "luxury" made from American upland) and may not be suitable for high–thread count sheets since they may end up feeling coarse after repeated washing. Pima is a fine, long-staple cotton that allows for a soft, strong weave and is usually more expensive than American upland cotton but less than Egyptian cotton. For a superior pima cotton sheet, look for the Supima cotton trademark, which indicates that this is an extra-long staple pima cotton grown in the United States. Egyptian cotton is the finest, longest staple of all. This cotton is grown in the Nile River valley. I am not alone in my opinion that pure, extra-long staple *Egyptian cotton* reigns supreme. There are many varieties of Egyptian cotton, so make sure that you are looking for an extra-long staple variety that's a highly graded quality. The Giza cotton variety is perhaps the most prized and is cherished for its exceptionally strong and long fibers.

There are also sheets made from linen and silk. Both are harder to find than cotton sheets and considerably more expensive. However, if taken care of, both linen and silk sheets can last a lifetime and can get better with every washing. Linen sheets wick off moisture and are great for hot summer nights. Silk sheets are warm and are therefore useful during the winter months.

- **Other Materials:** There are many other sheet options available today, including sheets made from cotton-polyester blends, bamboo blends, and synthetics like microfiber, which is a very popular option for inexpensive, no-wrinkle sheets. *Cotton-polyester blend sheets* are wrinkle-resistant, durable, and can cost much less than cotton sheets. A little polyester in a blend can go a long way, so be cautious. Sheets that are 90 percent cotton with 10 percent polyester will still provide breathability (important for not overheating while sleeping) but also wrinkle resistance. When the polyester content goes above 20 percent, you may find it hot and uncomfortable to sleep on. *Microfiber* is composed of very finely woven polyester fibers, defined by their thickness, or *denier*, the measurement of a fiber's thickness. For a material to be considered microfiber, it must be less than 1 denier in diameter. Because of its fineness, microfiber sheets tend to be very smooth, but the polyester fiber means—in general—it's not as breathable as cotton. *Bamboo* and *bamboo blends* (blended with cotton and other materials) use a base material that comes from the bamboo plant. Bamboo is known to be an environmentally friendly material, has antimicrobial properties, and can absorb moisture, so sheets made using this material can be a good choice for eco-conscious sleepers.

- **Weaves:** Most sheets are woven in one of two predominant methods: percale or sateen. Cotton, cotton blends, and synthetics can use either of these weaves. In *percale* *weave*, a continuous pattern of one warp thread over one weft thread, and then under the next weft, forms a one-over-one-under weave. The threads used in the weave help determine the overall strength and thickness of the sheet: thicker threads, woven tightly (higher thread count) will produce a thicker fabric. A percale weave tends to produce a crisper, cooler, and slightly more durable sheet. *Sateen weave* means that several warp threads go over one weft thread at a time to create a fabric with a satin-like, smooth finish. This weave creates a distinctive diagonal pattern if examined closely. Because of the nature of sateen weaving, sheets made with this process are generally both heavier and smoother but not as durable as a comparable percale sheet. With several warp threads going over each weave, they can be susceptible to snags and pulls.

- **Other Techniques:** *Jersey* and *flannel* are two other techniques used in making sheets. Jersey sheets are knitted (rather than woven) from cotton or cotton blends. Most often jersey sheets are made with one flat side and one piled side, a technique also used to make T-shirts. Flannel is usually made with a weft thread that is coarser than the warp thread, and it is often brushed after weaving to create a soft, almost cushy surface.

- **Thread length.** As I said earlier, *staple* refers to the length of the threads used to weave sheets. The longer the fiber, the better the weave—the material will be more durable and softer to the feel because the actual weave will be denser. Be careful, however, of high-thread count sheets made of inferior cotton fibers that may be shorter in length. They may be priced attractively, but the product can be stiff and poor in quality. Look for the words *long* or *extra-long staple cotton* or *Egyptian cotton* on sheet labels and packaging. Ultimately, it's important to be able to touch the sheets to ensure softness.

- **Thread count.** The thread count, which refers to the number of horizontal and vertical threads woven per square inch of fabric, is often thought to be one of the most important factors in determining softness and quality in a sheet. As I mentioned before, thread count is less important than type of fiber and length of fiber. With all other things being equal, a higher thread count usually translates to a softer and stronger sheet. Quality sheets will usually be between 200 and 1,000 thread count.

MATTRESSES 101

"A better night's sleep runs deep both physically and mentally," says Linda Klein, president of luxury mattress maker Charles P. Rogers. "You cannot achieve a restful sanctuary if you cringe at what's under the covers. Be proactive and select a mattress that's built to provide you and your partner with proper body alignment and the surface comfort you need and desire. Otherwise, that big muscle between your ears will never let go, relax, and recharge," she says. The right mattress can help muscles relax from their hard work holding up a heavy skeleton all day, and it can help reoxygenate the body. To help you find the best mattress for your sleep needs, here are Linda's expert tips:

- **Consider your body type, age, and lifestyle.** There are so many mattress options today, with various types of padding and coils and varying degrees of firmness from very soft to extra firm, that you should be able to find an exact match for your body. "As an older woman, I have body issues and pressure point areas that need to be addressed," says Linda. She prefers a mattress with firm inner springs of individual, hand-pocketed steel coils topped with layers of luxurious pure Talalay latex, wrapped around baby nano springs and finished with 100 percent natural wool. "This kind of mattress sculpts to my unique shape and supports my different body parts and weights." However, you can find comfortable mattresses that are a combination of coil springs and memory foam or gel foam, foam and latex, and other combinations. Whatever you choose, know that a good-quality mattress will pay you back with restful nights that prepare you for busy days.

- **Thickness doesn't always equal comfort.** "It's really about the quality and quantity of the materials used and how they are layered that results in a great mattress," says Linda. Old-school inner-spring mattresses are unstable and less firm than newer hybrid mattresses with individual, hand-pocketed, tempered-steel springs and quality surface materials. This kind of construction (and not the actual height of the mattress) accommodates different sleeping positions, including back, side, or tummy sleeping, or if we toss and turn a great deal.

- **Look for double-duty mattresses.** Many contemporary mattresses are built to provide unique body suspension for each partner's proper alignment. Look for those with the ability to customize each side if you and your partner have different sleep styles and preferences.

- **Seek long-term solutions.** The life of your mattress will vary based on the weight of the person or people sleeping on it. A good-quality steel inner-spring mattress should last you beyond a decade, while an all-foam mattress will perform for considerably less time, according to Linda. It's important to factor in how we change naturally or from traumatic events. Stress, wear, and tear can definitely impact our bodies and should not be ignored.

- **Quality counts.** Since most of us hope to sleep at least six to eight hours every day, buy a mattress that offers you the best-quality materials at the best value rather than a less expensive unit you throw away as it softens up and loses firmness. Spend your hard-earned dollars on the best mattress for you, with top-shelf materials, as close to the source who made it, for the best nights' sleep. Less expensive petrochemical foams break down much quicker than a stronger, more resilient latex, and an inner-spring unit with 50 percent less steel will sag more quickly over time. Your mattress selection will affect your health now and for the next ten years.

THE NIGHTSTAND

Your nightstand can become a source of stress if you allow it to become cluttered and unattractive. Although a small side table without a drawer can work perfectly well for guest bedrooms, your personal bedroom generally demands a nightstand with some kind of storage to get your necessary items (medicine, reading glasses, remote controls, etc.) out of sight while still keeping them accessible. Here are some of the ways I keep my nightstand looking good while at the same time doing its job of storing my things:

- **Keep accessories to a minimum.** Having a single, fresh-cut flower or stem of greenery displayed in a small-mouthed vase on your nightstand is an inexpensive and easy way to give your bedroom that vacation-like feel. This should be one of the few accessories displayed on the surface of your nightstand.

- **Use a remote box.** Televisions in bedrooms are a fact of life, unless you've switched over to viewing content through your laptop or other electronic device. If you have a television, you have a remote control, too. Having an additional, plastic electronic item sitting on your nightstand can suck all the design out of a space pretty quickly. If you don't have a drawer to put your remote in, a simple, decorative box with a hinged lid atop the nightstand is the next best alternative. The hinged lid will make accessing (and putting away) the remote easier.

- **The reading lamp is indispensable.** Keep your reading lamp on a dimmer so that you can adjust it to the perfect level in a darkened space. Ensure that the lampshade sits approximately at your eye level when you're seated in bed to prevent uncomfortable glare or poor illumination of your reading material.

- **Limit the number of books and magazines.** I love to read before going to bed. It helps me unwind and gets my brain prepared to shut off for the night, but reading material accumulates by my bedside, so I take the time to edit it down every day as part of my bed-making routine. I take any magazine that I'm done with to the recycling bin when I leave the room. For the size of my nightstand, two books and three magazines is about all it can handle before it starts veering away from soulful and charming and toward stressful and cluttered. You can only read one thing at a time, so try to limit your nightstand display to that one book and magazine you are actually reading at the moment. If you like to go back and forth between several books, put the ones not currently being read in your nightstand drawer so that they're easily accessible but out of sight.

MULTITASKING IN THE BEDROOM

What other purposes does your bedroom serve? The last thing most people want to do is turn a restful and romantic master bedroom retreat into a home office or as a last-resort storage area for things you don't want to be seen in public spaces. Here are my tips for keeping your bedroom restful and romantic.

- **Be smart about a bedroom desk.** I'm certainly not a fan of bringing everyday drudgery into the bedroom, but in some instances, there's no other place for a desk and the odds and ends of life. And, sometimes it is nice to have a quiet, private space to organize our thoughts or perhaps write a personal letter or journal entry. Just be diligent about keeping desk surfaces clear of paperwork and office supplies so that you're not staring at piles of bills and business reports (you'll never get a good night's sleep in that case!).

- **Add extra seating when possible.** If it's your get-away-from-it-all place, you may want to incorporate additional seating. There's nothing wrong with adding an upholstered lounge chair or two if you have the space. Other seating options like a chaise lounge, love seat, or sofa may help create an even calmer and more relaxing atmosphere. Ottomans can also be a particularly good choice, because they serve so many purposes; they can be used as additional seating, as a surface for a board game, or as a dining surface. Or you can even use them for their intent and rest your tired feet!

- **Make sure all systems are go!** Review the room's ventilation, acoustics, and system controls. The room should be ventilated correctly. Place your bed away from air vents and make sure you have access to fresh air. If possible, add extra insulation between walls, install an upgraded pad under your carpet or rug, add floor-to-ceiling drapery, and a fabric headboard to minimize distracting external sounds. In addition, if your budget permits, add a wireless speaker or concealed speakers at key areas for a sound system. Install drapery treatments that stack or can be pushed past the glass of the windows to maximize views.

- **Include sun control.** Wood blinds and other shade devices help to ensure nighttime serenity. Drapery panels should overlap at least four inches at center draws so that a "blackout" environment can be maintained when you want to snooze. Make sure drapery panels have a top-notch liner; nothing looks rougher or more unfinished—the antithesis of tranquility—than unlined fabric. It lacks the polish a truly luxurious room possesses. Lined drapery generally also hangs better for a neater aesthetic and tends to do a better job controlling both sound and light. For particularly light-sensitive sleepers, ensure blackout lining is incorporated into your drapery.

INDULGE YOUR PERSONAL SPACES

The world's best hotel rooms often feature original art pieces from the region and local interest magazines, replete with beautiful images, so that a guest feels a connection with the city they are visiting. For your own room, remember that a favorite painting, family photograph, art book, or a limited collection of your favorite books helps create the atmosphere of a personal and unique retreat. Include such special items in your decorating scheme so you feel connected and at peace.

Once you have the main elements in place, you can have fun adding little touches and extras to make your bedroom a luxurious cocoon that you may never want to leave. Keep in mind that these additions should not bring clutter into your understated retreat; their purpose is simply to help you relax and de-stress.

In first-class hotel rooms, the following techniques are often used:

- Three-way switch at entry for bedside lamp.

- Closet light that turns on automatically when door is opened.

- Bedside reading lights that are individually controlled.

- Dimmer controls on everything!

- A remote-controlled gas fireplace brings the warmth—literal and symbolic—of a fire, without the need to tend it or worry that it's really out.

- For the ultimate combination of high- and low-tech luxury, invest in sconces in which you place remote-controlled LED candles. These ingenious little things give off the flickering glow of wax candles, and you can turn them on or off at the touch of a remote.

- Don't forget the potpourri, fragrance diffuser, or highly fragranced fresh flowers, such as peonies. Find a scent that puts you in a mellow mood, and make it your bedroom's signature scent—don't use it in any other room!

- Lightly spritz your sheets with a room fragrance before you go to bed. It makes getting into bed extra special.

- Invest in a small, easy-to-transport tray that can accommodate a small snack, water decanter, and glass to address bedtime hunger and thirst.

BATHROOMS

One of the great luxuries of staying at a great resort is access to a huge, well-appointed bathroom. At home, we spend so much time in this space that it's worth it to have your own bathroom evoke the appealing features of the one in your favorite hotel, even if your room does not match its proportions. The time, energy, and resources you devote to designing your bathroom will pay you back many times over. It's one of the first rooms you see in the morning and one of the last you see before you go to bed. And if you live with someone else, or have a hectic family life, it's often the only place where you can escape and rejuvenate for a few minutes . . . so make it beautiful, organized, and reflective of you so that you get those few moments of relaxation when you're in it.

- FOCAL POINT. People often choose to make the tub, soaking tub, or shower the focal point of their bathroom. A great shower or a freestanding tub can make a statement and add drama to a bathroom. Either can be pleasant to look at and functional—water is a great reset at the beginning or end of a hectic day, so why not make bathing or showering an amazing experience? Plus, having a clear focal point usually facilitates order in a space, which then translates to a more relaxed environment.

- RUGS. While most bath mats are great for soaking up the moisture from your feet when you step out of the shower or bathtub, consider a rug or rug runner (the kind you would use in any other room in the house) for your bathroom vanity area and in your powder rooms. The right rug in a bathroom can deliver a lot of bang for the buck in the looks department. In fact, at many luxury properties, the bathrooms are often outfitted with handwoven runners that you'd normally see in high-end residential hallways.

They add a special touch of unexpected luxury in front of their bathroom vanities. Every time I brushed my teeth in hotels with this setup, it felt special! As a result, I now try to place beautiful rug runners in my home bathrooms whenever possible.

- LIGHTING. Make sure there is ample lighting in the bathroom. Must-haves include a lighted makeup mirror, wall sconces, overhead lighting at the vanity, and lighting in the tub area.

- FURNITURE. Embrace real furniture in the bathroom. Top resorts have used beautiful furniture that would look great in any room in your house in their bathrooms. A lovely chair, bench, or side table can add a warm and welcoming accent to all of that metal, marble, and tile that many of us have. Even a small chest of drawers can look inviting—and offers handy storage, too.

- STORAGE. Keep grooming paraphernalia and makeup out of sight. We all need our "products" to feel the best we can, but we don't need to look at them all the time. These products are meant to be used on *you*, not used as a home accessory. Have a shelf in the linen closet, a drawer in the vanity, or a shelf in the wall-mounted cabinet to keep these kinds of functional items out of sight.

- FLORA. A single, fresh blossom in a vase on the vanity is a simple-to-achieve yet luxurious finishing touch.

I freely admit that I have a strong personal preference for neutral and all-white bathrooms. For me, powder rooms are where bolder and more intensely hued colors can be showcased. A light neutral or all-white bathroom will reflect rather than absorb light, creating naturally refreshing space. It looks clean, and because you can see every speck of dirt, you can easily maintain its pristine quality. Heavily patterned accent tiles and those in vibrant colors can initially seem like a great idea, but I find that they are expensive additions that too often reflect the trend of the moment and date a bathroom quickly—I forgo them and recommend that you do, too, if you want a timeless design that will endure until you're simply ready for a change.

This monochromatic decor conveys not only a sense of cleanliness and freshness but also simplicity and purity—a place where all the stresses of the day are washed away. Neutral and white walls are particularly useful in baths that already have great views of the outdoors. The vibrant greenery of plants and trees or the various tones of blue from a body of water look that much lovelier when presented through the "frame" of a wall that's not competing with it for attention.

Don't fall into the trap of thinking that all whites are created equal. An all-white bathroom can look cold and sterile if you don't choose carefully and end up with a white with too much blue in its undertone. To determine if you have the right white, tape a swatch of your shade to several of the walls of the room you are looking to paint. Examine it during the daytime (with no artificial lights on) while it's both naturally lit and in shadow. If you see hints of blue in the swatch, your shade may have blue in its undertone.

Look at the swatch with your artificial lights on, too, during both the daytime and at night to make sure that you like what you see. Artificial lights tend to cast a warmer light, so they aren't necessarily useful for detecting the blue undertone in a white shade, but it's still a useful exercise to ensure you like what you see.

Of course, you can learn a lot about what is in a paint color by talking to the salesperson, which is why it might be a good idea to go to a dedicated paint store if you feel nervous about making a selection. The staff can steer you to colors that have, more or less, the key undertones you are seeking.

When you find the right shade of white, your room feels warm and relaxing. It's helpful to know where and when the sun comes into rooms when selecting paint color. You may not think to choose paint with a compass in your hand (most smartphones feature them), but morning or afternoon sun does have an effect on how paint color appears on walls. For instance, there's a difference between serene whites and antiseptic whites and how they appear in south- and north-facing rooms. North-facing rooms can be challenging in general because they tend to be darker overall than sunnier, south-facing rooms:

- Cool whites, with blue or black base pigments, can look crisp in south-facing rooms where the color of the natural light is a little warmer and brighter than north-facing rooms. The warmer-colored, natural light has an ameliorating impact on the cooler-toned whites, counterbalancing their undertone. Warmer-toned whites can also work beautifully in south-facing rooms, but be careful not to go too warm since you'll already be contending with the warm-colored, natural light, which may turn a very warm white yellow.

- Warm whites, with yellow or red undertones, work well in north-facing rooms that tend to be darker and where the color of the natural light is a little cooler. Cooler whites can appear clinical and uninviting in these situations.

LEARN FROM VERN:
LITTLE LUXURIES

HAND SOAP. Put out nice-smelling liquid hand soap in a simple, beautiful dispenser. This allows you to have a brief moment to enjoy something pleasant smelling each time you wash your hands.

HAND CREAM. It's nice to have one beautiful bottle of lotion to soothe your hands. Choose something that is already in an attractive package—or transfer your favorite lotion into a beautiful dispenser, which can be found at every price point. It's extra nice if it blends in with your bath decor.

HEATED TOWEL RACK. There's nothing more luxurious than a fluffy warm towel. An investment in a heated towel rack will repay you many times over each time you envelop yourself in a heated towel.

PRODUCT DISPLAY. I always turn my product labels forward if they're exposed. It takes only a second, and I find that turning all the labels forward helps to create a sense of organization that's ultimately less distracting. Simply turning my shampoo, conditioner, liquid soap, and shaving gel dispensers with their labels forward makes the niche and shower look neater immediately. Of course, you can always go one step further and invest in some nice-looking dispensers without labels, but I'm often too short on time and need to make do with the dispensers my products already come in.

MATERIALS FOR THE BATHROOM

• WALL TILE

Install cohesive, simple floor to ceiling and inside corner to inside corner whenever possible so that you are addressing an entire wall. This will help limit the visual distractions and lend a richer and calmer feel to your bathroom space. It also makes your walls less susceptible to humidity staining. I also prefer the fresh and timeless look of an uninterrupted expanse of a single tile. It's visually restful, and it offers up the tranquil feeling of a luxury hotel. Remember, it's important that every room has a clear focal point to remain restful. Make sure tiles aren't begging for as much attention as a great view or a dramatic soaking tub. If you don't have the space or the means to install a freestanding soaking tub as a focal point, a well-designed shower also makes a wonderful focal point of the room.

• FLOOR TILE

Outside the shower, select larger tile to reduce the number of grout joints and keep those joints as tight as possible. I love the look of both porcelain ceramic tile and natural stone like marble and limestone; these are timeless materials. For high-traffic bathrooms and minimal maintenance, it's hard to beat porcelain ceramic tile, which won't require sealing and resealing to prevent staining. For less public bathrooms, like your master bathroom, it may feel more resort-like to splurge on a marble or limestone that will feel special each time you set foot in your sanctuary of a space. In either case, keep it simple and let the tile speak for itself. Celebrate its natural beauty.

• COUNTERTOPS

It's hard to beat the zero-maintenance and variety of looks that quartz affords. I particularly love the Cambria quartz collection, which features some designs that nearly duplicate the look of marble without all the associated maintenance and worry over scratching and staining.

• VANITIES

For master bathrooms and bathrooms designed to service bedrooms, always employ vanities with some degree of built-in storage—preferably drawers because they give you more options for organizing your stuff and having it right where you need it, when you need it. The ability to cleanly and neatly put away a hair dryer and some toiletries is invaluable toward maintaining a clean and clutter-free bathroom environment.

• SINKS AND PORCELAIN ITEMS

When it comes to selecting your porcelain items, such as your toilets and sinks, avoid colors and stick to white, off-white, or bone. You'll rarely go to a luxury hotel or resort that uses any other ceramic color because they're trying to convey cleanliness, which always helps ease the mind, especially in the bedroom and the bathroom. Additionally, these items tend to last until it's time for a renovation (and sometimes even beyond one), so keeping them in fresh and timeless white or bone ultimately saves you money down the road. They'll also go with almost any color and decor change, so repainting your bathroom won't mean replacing these items, too!

I encourage people to design their master bathrooms to achieve that same feeling of calm and relaxation. For instance, an undermount sink (one that is installed beneath the countertop) is a traditional way to install bathroom sinks and is helpful for ease of cleaning. But I also love large vessel sinks because they can feel so luxurious. For me, a vessel sink is special and gives me the feeling of being at a spa or somewhere significant. And why shouldn't getting ready for the day feel like that always! A deep and wide vessel sink also contains all my splash when I wash my face, eliminating the extra step of wiping water off the vanity top.

• PLUMBING FIXTURES

There are endless choices and many new style trends, so you could spend a lot of time deciding on what faucets, drawer pulls, and other fixtures you want in your bath. Matte finishes are very popular and up-to-the-minute; they work well in larger rooms because they absorb light and make space feel more intimate. Matte chrome, nickel, and gold especially enhance this feeling. Matte gold and rose gold also seem to be having a moment, and some homeowners find these new choices particularly romantic and glamorous. My personal preference is classic polished chrome or the more transitional (a compromise between modern and traditional) polished nickel. These choices look good no matter the style of your bath; are easy to keep clean and require no special treatment, just a good wipe; and look luxe and low-key at the same time.

Polished finishes are great for expanding the sense of space because they take light and reflect it back into the environment, expanding the perception of volume. For this reason, they especially work well in smaller spaces, where their reflective quality adds a feeling of spaciousness, but I love using them in bathrooms of all sizes. Be sure to keep all metal finishes in your bathroom the same to enhance the sense of calm and reduce distraction.

Rain showerheads, whether coming from the wall or installed in the ceiling of a shower, always feel relaxing and luxurious to me, and nearly every luxury resort has them. In fact, when traveling, I used to think, *I'm really going to miss this terrific shower,* until I realized I could put one in my own bathroom! I love the way the downpour of water elevates an everyday event into a special time. Showers are one of the few times when you have a moment all to yourself, when you're not answering a phone or replying to e-mail—so make the most of them! However, the one caveat about rain showerheads is for people who do not wash their hair on a daily basis. Because this design offers a deluge of glorious, all-encompassing wetness, it may not be so glorious if you are trying to keep your hair dry while getting the rest of you clean.

• TOWELS

To create that sense of cleanliness and calm, employ large, fluffy white towels like the best hotels do. This may seem contrary to what you think you should be doing because white tends to show dirt easier, but their sparkling, clean look can instantly elevate the look of a space and convey that it's neat and taken care of. When I was first working professionally, I could finally afford to buy a few nice things for my tiny apartment. I had noticed my sister's high-end towels, which felt both thick and luxurious. I ordered the same ones, but in an earthy brown because I thought it gave my bathroom a clean-lined, masculine aesthetic. They were great—fluffy, soft, and absorbent. But even when they were freshly laundered, their color made them look dirty or at least not invitingly clean. They also began to fade with repeated laundering, and it was soon clear that I used some towels far more than others. I never made that mistake again.

Your bath towels should ideally be laundered every three days of consecutive, daily use. Hand towels may need to be laundered more frequently, perhaps every two days with frequent use, because they're often drying hands that may not be completely clean. Additionally, white towels can also be bleached if necessary, when a particularly tough stain appears. For removal of makeup or at-home hair dye stains, keep older or colored towels accessible but stored out of sight. Buy the best you can, preferably Egyptian, Turkish, or pima cotton, which have long fibers for a soft feel and excellent absorbency. These are the kind of towels you'll find at the finest spas and resorts. Just like your sheets, your towels will need to be replaced eventually. With normal, daily use, most towels will need to be replaced every two years. The true barometer, however, is the loss of absorbency. Once they've lost their ability to absorb efficiently, you should get new ones.

• MIRRORS

In my new beach house, I ordered TruStile doors with mirrors integrated into them for all my closets so I do not have to figure out where to locate a full-length mirror. This is an idea that I've employed with bathroom doors as well. Not only does this free up real estate, but a mirrored door makes the room feel lighter, brighter, and more spacious. And a full-length mirror feels especially nice. In a tight bathroom or bedroom, you want the wall for storage, so putting the mirror on your door or integrating it as a panel on the door is both functional and space-saving.

• LIGHTING

Let's face it—one of the great appeals of the bathroom is that it's the one place that lets you be you, so getting the right lighting is really important. It used to be that a fixture or two installed close to the vanity mirror, and maybe a light in the shower, was the extent of the decisions we had to make about the bathroom. Not anymore. Today we have a dizzying array of choices for the kind of lighting we use and for the placements of those lights, so we need to think about what matters most.

For me, there are two top considerations when it comes to lighting in the bath. First, I want to be able to see what I'm doing when I'm shaving and getting ready for the day. Second, I want to be enveloped with a feeling of calmness that comes with the territory at a high-end spa. Therefore, I want specific task lighting near the mirror to front light in a bright, shadow-free way. Lighting in the remainder of the room is ambient and should be softer and dimmable. What can be more relaxing than a hot shower or long soak in a tub surrounded by the soft, warm glow of subdued lighting?

Many stylish baths today feature a statement chandelier or pendant fixture, which is a larger-scaled light hanging from the ceiling from a rod, chain, or wire, and it's easy to see why. They add a feeling of real luxury in small spaces and grandeur in larger spaces—and make no mistake, bathrooms are getting larger and larger in the new construction of homes and high-end hotel properties. A statement light fixture in a bathroom can make it feel like a destination.

Make sure that the bulbs you install in all of your bathroom lighting are dimmable so that you can adjust the brightness according to your need or your mood. Keep in mind that the movement toward LED may require the installation of special dimmers. The advantage of LEDs is that they last for years (roughly twenty years or more), so while they seem pricey when you buy them, in the long run, they save you money because you rarely replace them and they are cheaper to run, while also saving you the hassle of getting out the ladder to change them. That's one less thing on your to-do list!

Avoid compact fluorescent lighting (CFL) in all spaces you will actually be spending time in if possible. The light quality tends to be harsh, and, though you'll save money on energy just like you will with LEDs, the light will make those environments less pleasurable to inhabit. With LED technology, there's very little reason to select CFLs in my opinion—even in laundry and other utility rooms.

STORAGE FOR THE BATH

Small spaces like bathrooms can present storage woes. Here are some tips to keep storage in your bathroom functional and aesthetically pleasing:

- **Opt for drawers.** As we've discussed, in baths that are adjacent to bedrooms, having a vanity with drawers is a priority. Drawers (rather than cabinets with doors) let you organize your stuff and stash it from view.

- **Don't overlook the medicine cabinet.** In the smallest spaces, one of the best storage solutions is the old-fashioned medicine cabinet. I've kept my toothbrush and toothpaste out of sight in a flush-mounted version, although surface mounts also work and can look great. Some medicine cabinets offer full-length vertical storage, too, so they are good double-duty solutions.

- **Basket case:** In larger baths, some people add space with storage caddies or baskets. In tight quarters, especially, open baskets are more of a nuisance than a solution. So, whether your bathroom space is large or small, find and use baskets and caddies with fitted or hinged lids.

- **Consistency is key.** If you must store towels on open shelving, take the time to roll or fold them consistently so they stack neatly on shelves. It's uninviting to be confronted with an unruly pile of towels crumpled on a shelf.

CHILDREN'S ROOMS

It's natural to think *cheerful* when putting together a bedroom for your child, but *cheerful* doesn't have to translate to a roomful of loud primary colors on the walls and bedding. Your children may need a refuge, too, and hyperpigmented orange, red, or purple walls tend not to be restful. One solution for creating that sense of calm and relaxation in their rooms, while addressing a desire for bright, saturated colors, is to keep the color of your kids' rooms' walls neutral and let their toys, bedding, artwork, and decorative accessories provide the room with their desired brightness and saturation. If your child really wants to put bright, saturated color on the walls, ameliorate the intense impact with a simple, alternating stripe that folds a neutral into the pattern. You could also consider painting the interior of their closet or perhaps the back of any open shelving (remember to keep those shelves neat!). These smaller spaces aren't staring you in the face constantly, and painting them a vibrant color can turn them into jewel boxes and magical moments.

My kids also have designated toy areas. We have a family rule about these storage places: every toy is put back when you are finished playing with it. We've had them help clean up their toys since they were toddlers, so they are used to it and understand that it not only helps keep the house clean and calm but also allows them to easily locate a desired item when they want to play with it. For our family, this has been an important habit to form because the kids' rooms are heavily used and could easily fall into chaos. Plus, with the toys safely tucked away, I don't have to worry about tripping over them in the dark. How many of you have ever stepped on a LEGO barefoot? It can be extremely painful!

As with the rest of the house, when things have a designated spot, it makes keeping the space clean and uncluttered so much easier, and you also know where to find what you are looking for when you need or want it. A toy box or chest accomplishes the same goal. Furniture with plenty of smart storage, such as a nightstand with doors and drawers, can help, too. If space is really at a premium, look into a bed with built-in storage or get under-the-bed storage containers, which will hold all but the bulkiest toys and keep them neatly out of sight and organized when not in use.

BEFORE YOU CHECK OUT . . .

- Don't let clutter take over your private spaces. Think about why you may love hotel rooms so much: they represent in their most basic form, an uncluttered and crisp bed and bath. That's the feeling you want to take home with you, and not the generic artwork on the wall or the tiny soaps and miniature shampoo bottles!

- Make art personal. Artwork, whether that's a painting or photos, sculpture or framed needlework, can be indulgent and deeply personal in private spaces. Surround yourself with artwork that speaks to your personal journey and memories in private spaces.

- Create an environment that speaks to your inner self.

  » Private spaces should be where you are free to be yourself, no matter how unconventional, unusual, or unique. These kinds of spaces are the ultimate for replenishing and relaxing your spirit because you don't necessarily have to compromise to meet the functional needs or aesthetic preferences of other household members.

  » Create at least one space in your home where you can peacefully escape and get a moment to yourself, like your bedroom or bath. Luxury hotels often will create spaces off the main lobbies where guests can have a moment of privacy. Having this kind of space, and keeping it free of chaos and technology, can be vital toward making your home a place you look forward to returning to.

- Design to appeal to all of your senses. The small, sensual touches such as fresh flowers or plants, scented candles or fragrance diffusers, atmospheric music, and art add immeasurably to creating that private retreat space that beckons you.

CHAPTER 5
AT WORK AND PLAY

We do so much of our living and gathering in our kitchens, media rooms, and home offices. Even some utilitarian rooms, like laundry and mudrooms, see their fair share of daily activity. Why shouldn't these rooms also reenergize, restore, and relax you? They should! Hardworking rooms deserve special treatment because daily tasks should elevate us just as much as a luxurious bedroom or living room does.

KITCHENS

You've heard all the clichés: "The kitchen is the heart of the home"; "The kitchen is where my family and friends gather"; "I love having people around me while I cook." As a designer, I have many clients who ask me for help designing their dream kitchen that will fulfill these very desires, and I am happy to oblige—my own family uses our kitchen as a gathering spot.

Reality check. The kitchen has an important and primary purpose: the storage, preparation, and cleanup associated with food. Do you see the kitchen as your luxury retreat? In its current condition, do you even *want* to see it? As we strive for restraint and simplicity in order to live less-stressed lives, it's time to take a fresh look at kitchens and learn to apply strategies that help us enjoy our kitchens not just as utilitarian public spaces but as beautiful spaces where we can unwind and make a cup of tea or enjoy a conversation. None of which is to say that the kitchen can't be a beautiful part of the home. It can and should, but its beauty should also respect and reflect your need for ease of preparation, not to mention storage and cleanup.

Two principles guide the design of top hotel kitchens: efficiency and endurance. When a new hotel is planned, a good kitchen designer will take into account motion studies to determine the room's layout, so that the value of the chef's time is maximized. Your kitchen should take the value of *your* time into account when determining the placement of appliances in relation to each other, and to counter space and the placement of cabinetry in relation to preparation, serving, and cleanup areas. The fewer the steps you must take, and the fewer trips you need to make to fetch an ingredient, utensil, or serving implement, the better. In the hotel world, time is money; for the rest of us, time is a luxury we all want more of. Simple, efficient kitchen design can give us that luxury.

Outfitting a hotel kitchen is an exercise in procuring the best appliances and equipment to withstand constant use. Aesthetics are not part of the equation, although many people find the sleek, cool look of gleaming industrial kitchens very appealing. But even if you're not such a person, you can benefit from a kitchen with durable countertops, cabinets, and appliances. There is no substitute for top quality in the kitchen. It's the workhorse of the home, and its components need to be good-looking and long-lasting, including the pots, pans, and gadgets.

A luxury kitchen, therefore, doesn't have to mean Carrara marble everywhere (which can be difficult to care for, anyway) or counters and cabinets full of all manner of the latest appliances. A truly luxurious kitchen is one that

- Reflects your taste and style—and visually delights you when you enter.

- Has ease of meal preparation as its highest priority, whether you consider yourself a cook or not.

- Features countertops that are beautiful to look at yet are super durable, low maintenance, and easy to clean, such as quartz, a personal favorite of mine.

- Has easy-care flooring, such as ceramic or porcelain tiles that do not need to be sealed, installed in large modules that are tightly set to minimize unsightly and difficult-to-keep-clean grout lines (kept to ⅛ inch or less, if possible), or wood floors with the proper finish to withstand high traffic and dropped utensils.

- Is loaded with the right cabinet inserts that make it easy to keep things organized. Go as high as you can with your kitchen cabinets even if you have really high ceilings (at least up to twelve feet). If there's space between the top of your wall-hung cabinets and the ceiling (and ideally there shouldn't be), keep this area clear of decorative objects and fake plants, which will only gather dust and act as unnecessary visual pollution.

- Has smart cabinet door solutions, like those with solid doors or those fitted with mirrors instead of transparent glass. Both options allow you to maximize your storage without having to worry about displaying your things neatly. If you have plenty of cabinet storage space, glass cabinet doors are a helpful way to break up a mass of solid cabinet fronts and a beautiful way to showcase your special and attractive items. Steer clear of glass cabinet doors, however, when upper cabinet space is limited— they're gorgeous, but you have to keep the contents looking great at all times (think decorative china and glass, not cans of noodle soup and bags of chips). There is often simply too much potential for visual chaos in situations where you're already pressed for storage.

- Has every appliance and piece of equipment you need, but *not one thing more*, stored off the countertop whenever possible.

- Has an easily located binder containing all your appliance manuals and warranties. You can also take down appliance numbers to pull up online manuals when you need them or digitize your manuals so that you don't have to provide space for physical ones.

- Is relaxed and welcoming. Whether you're on a limited budget or an unlimited one, there are two steps you can take that can help deliver a more relaxing transformation to the room. One of them, the most important, doesn't cost a dime. Conduct an inventory of your kitchen, and as you go through your things, ask yourself questions, such as when was the last time I used my risotto maker? If your answer was "Sometime last year," or, more likely, "Never," or, most likely, "I have a risotto maker?!" it's time to get rid of it. Seriously, unless you use an appliance at least monthly, chances are it's taking up precious space in your kitchen and giving you little in return. Sell, donate, or dispose of it. Similarly, appraise your utensils. Do you really need four identical spatulas? If you do, fine, great—keep them. But if you don't, free up space by getting rid of the excess.

- Has attractive hardware. A quick way to refresh your kitchen and give it a luxe vibe is to change the hardware on the cabinets. There's a multitude of choices on the market, and you can most certainly find a style that reflects you. I like to stick to the same style and size of pulls on both cabinet doors and drawers whenever possible. I find that it's yet another way of minimizing visual clutter and distraction in the kitchen.

NEAT + CLEAN = A STRESS-FREE KITCHEN

A clean and clutter-free kitchen will truly be the heart of your home because you'll love it rather than hate it. Dirty dishes in the sink, spices and oils cluttering up countertops, even too many open baskets of produce make me feel more like dinner reservations than whipping up a family meal. Here are some practices that will keep chaos out of your kitchen.

- END YOUR DAY WITH A CLEAN KITCHEN. Place your dishes, glasses, and cutlery directly into the dishwasher as soon as you're done with them. I like to run the dishwasher right after dinner, which allows me to unload it before I go to bed, eliminating one more thing I have to deal with during our busy morning. Plus, the last thing you want to encounter first thing in the morning is a sink full of dirty dishes or a full dishwasher to unload! There are so many better ways to start the day.

- KEEP APPLIANCES OUT OF SIGHT. Get rid of small appliances and other kitchen items that you don't use. We all accumulate kitchen stuff we don't need over time. Hide small appliances that you use frequently (toasters, blenders, and so on) behind doors or appliance garages (a customized countertop compartment sometimes fitted with a rolltop or tambour door specifically designed to conceal large kitchen appliances, but keep them handy). If you're lucky enough to have one, store appliances in an adjacent butler's pantry or a large walk-in pantry. Integrate your microwave into cabinetry. Microwave drawers are a great counter-clearing option. For tighter spaces, consider having your microwave above your range as a microwave/hood combination.

- KEEP IT PRACTICAL. Everyday dishware, glassware, and cutlery should be beautiful but dishwasher safe. Hotels and top resorts choose great-looking glass and tableware in the same way—they can stand up to high-heat dishwashers without wearing out. Choose a price point so that when something breaks, it's not a tragedy. A single-color palette that brings you joy will work as long as you stick to it. Consider adding in colorful serving platters or salad plates (for instance) to the mix—they will make basic white dishes look different for entertaining throughout the year.

- UNDERMOUNT THE SINK. It's much easier to keep an undermounted sink clean compared to a top-mounted one, which is not flush with the counter, so that food and general kitchen grime can lodge in the crevice along the edge of the sink and the counter. Farmhouse sinks, very popular today, can have some of the same issues, with dirt getting stuck between the sides of the sink and the counter.

- CHOOSE A STURDY SINK MATERIAL. Stainless steel is popular because it's easy to keep clean, and like the name says, it's resistant to staining. Enameled cast iron is lovely, but the enamel can chip if a heavy pot hits it too hard, and light colors like white and bone are prone to stains. Colored enamels like black or brown may not show stains as easily, but you may tire of the color more quickly than you would a basic white. And while a deeply colored sink can look modern, they certainly don't say "clean" as loudly and clearly as white does. An integrated sink in a solid surface (like Corian) can also be very easy to clean but could be prone to chipping.

- STOW CLEANING IMPLEMENTS. Sponges, cloths, and scrubbers should be off the countertop. Consider a built-in pull-down in front of your sink or a nearby special drawer for these items. A special caddy that's mountable to the inside of your sink cabinet door is a smart and convenient solution, too.

TECH ROOMS AND HOME OFFICES

My husband and I both work from home, so having a home office isn't an option; it's a necessity. We each need an office in our home, in addition to conference space, an area to showcase and photograph products, and a full resource library. In fact, I'm unusual in that almost every portion of my home could be considered part of my work space since it's all a critical and indispensable component of my design work. My business is basically all about the home! Also, as an interior designer who's been fortunate enough to be able to build a brand through product design as well, I test out each and every fabric, light fixture, and any other product (no matter how small) by living with it in my own home, under typical family life conditions replete with dogs and kids, before it hits the market.

In the twenty-first century, *home office* has increasingly come to mean a room packed with all manner of electronics, business machines, and other gadgets. Moreover, no matter what you do for a living, e-mails and text messages have found their way into practically every square inch of everyone's house and into every minute of everyone's life. It's become a fact of our modern, digital world where anyone and everyone can reach you through your phone and laptop. So, wherever you are standing, you're in your office! I often think of these home work spaces not so much as offices but as tech rooms. Mine has certainly become like that. Integrating boxy equipment, endless cords, and routers into a highly functional space that still looks like it is part of a gracious home can be a challenge.

Fortunately, as working from home has become more and more a fact of life, the marketplace has introduced many products that allow us to make our work spaces as attractive as they are functional, and the increasing ubiquity of wireless connections lets us cut the cords that used to snake around our rooms like invasive vines.

- GO SMALL. Consider a laptop computer. Not only do they take up less space than a desktop model, many models are remarkably unobtrusive in design, blending well with different decors. They are also super easy to stow away when you're done working so you don't have to look at a computer when you are trying to do something non-digital.

- CLOUD THE ISSUE. Let the computer's memory and cloud storage replace your file cabinet. Scan documents and file them in a virtual file to reduce paperwork and the need for bulky file folders and cabinets. Digitizing can make all those papers so much more manageable.

- PAY ONLINE. Go electronic with your bills. Reducing the paper in your mailbox will help reduce clutter management, and paying online helps reduce the need for envelopes, pens, checkbooks, and stamps.

- MULTITASK. Seek out multipurpose equipment, such as a combination fax/printer/scanner to save space and reduce the administrative look of your office.

- STOW IT, DON'T SHOW IT. Designate a drawer on your desk to contain pens, sticky notes, stamps, paper clips, rubber bands, and other small office items. The small stuff can still look busy, especially when organized in desktop pencil holders or baskets. To remedy that, if you have limited drawer space, make sure that whatever desktop storage you use is opaque to reduce visual distraction.

LAUNDRY ROOMS

Laundry rooms are prone to disorder because the very act of placing clothes in the washer and then the dryer—especially if you have more than one load to do—seems to naturally create piles. The accoutrements of cleaning and sorting also get caught up in the mess. Here are some ways to keep the laundry room fresh and functional:

- TAKE IMMEDIATE ACTION. It may take practice, but if you fold and hang items as soon as you take them out of your dryer, and then store them in the appropriate closet, you will find piles of laundry do not add up. It's a great habit that in the long run saves you time and annoyance.

- KEEP IT SIMPLE. Have a series of neutral, coordinated hampers for your dirty clothes—one for whites, one for colors, and one for delicate items. Again, not everything is meant to be a design statement or should be calling out for attention. Some items are perfectly fine to remain as primarily functional. Laundry hampers, in my opinion, should fall into that category.

- IRON UP. Install a wall-hung iron and ironing board holder near your laundry area. This gets them off other surfaces. With the iron close at hand, you can press those fresh but slightly damp pillowcases and sheets as soon as they come out of the dryer.

- HANG IT. Have uniform clothes hangers handy in a wood tone or neutral color like gray, black, or white. I love the look of uniform hangers; they help convey a neat, pulled-together look. Clothes hangers are not expensive, but they serve as the foundation for an organized look to your closets. I recommend using the same hangers throughout the entire house so that they can flow freely from space to space without adding visual distraction to any of your closets. When I have items that need to be hung for drying purposes, it always helps that my hangers in the laundry room match those in the closet. This allows clothes to transfer back into the closets without an extra step of switching hangers. And by keeping them all to a uniform color, you remove them as an unintended and distracting design statement.

- SINK IN. If space and budget permit, have a sink for presoaking and hand-washing delicate items.

- GO PRO. The laundry's storage closet should contain useful items the pros use, including a drying rack, a steamer (fabulous for shirts), and any cleaning products that you buy in bulk.

- CLEAR IT. Keep the work surface for folding clothes free of any objects.

- HIDE IT. Placing detergent and softener behind closed doors reduces the visual noise. There's already enough going in these spaces visually. Remember, you want to display and showcase purposefully so that only the things that you love are out to see. All other items should go behind closed storage whenever possible.

- CLEAN IT. Finally, and most important, don't forget to keep your washer and dryer clean. Nothing spoils the pleasure of looking at and smelling fresh clean clothes and linens more than looking at a scummy soap dispenser in the washer, crusted with drying detergent, or a lint-clogged dryer filter—which goes beyond unattractive and into the realm of fire hazard.

STORAGE AREAS

Storage is a fact of life for many of us. Here are a few pro tips that keep storage from taking over your home and your life:

- **Designate one room in the house for storage.** That room should never be your foyer or bedroom, which are critical spaces for creating that sense of relaxation. Of course, being able to walk into every room of your home and be relaxed by what you see is the ultimate goal, but containing the disarray to one area is a much better, temporary approach than having a little bit of disorganization everywhere. By having all but one room in your house pulled together, you allow for a sense of ease throughout the rest of your home. It's best if that disorganized room has a door on it, but even if it doesn't, you at least keep "projects" to one space so that you can chip away at the clutter, with a goal of eventually eliminating the need for that kind of space.

- **Create a system.** A storage room does not have to be impeccable but it can and should have some system of organizing what's in it, even if it is on clearly marked shelves or storage containers. That way you can at least have some sense of what is where and retrieve it (or replace it) when necessary.

- **Use large closed storage.** If you don't have a spare room to designate, utilize a great storage piece, an extra kitchen cabinet, or even a solid bin that can be tucked away somewhere.

- **Take inventory.** Spring and fall are great times to do this. How many times have you come across a box in your basement and realized you haven't opened it since you moved in? Once or twice a year, review the contents of your storage area and decide whether you really want to keep what you have squirreled away. Pretend you're getting ready for a move, and ask yourself, Do I really want to take this with me? If the answer is no, then don't wait for that move—get rid of the unnecessary article now. When the time comes that you actually are moving, you will have made that awful job so much easier. Storing things, even in our own homes, still costs something: our valuable time and energy to manage it. Remember, that's time that you could be relaxing in your home instead!

OUT OF SIGHT DOESN'T MEAN UNSIGHTLY!

Just because a room is utilitarian doesn't mean it shouldn't be organized and pleasant to be in when you're looking for your power drill or paint or storing your bikes after a ride. The key to keeping storage spaces like basements, attics, and sheds neat and organized—and, therefore, more able to fulfill their intended purpose of storage—is to make efficient use of labeled shelves and storage receptacles such as plastic tubs. The same is true of workshops.

- Label shelves and storage containers so that you know where to find things when you need them and where to put them back when you are finished with them.

- Store items according to how often you use them. Keep the things you use most often in easy reach.

- Buy identical storage tubs so that the space looks like a unified whole. This is calming to the eye. Also, try to select neutral-colored tubs in gray, beige, black, or soft shades of white to prevent drawing attention to an unintended design statement.

BEFORE YOU CHECK OUT . . .

- Hardworking spaces can look great and still function efficiently.

  » Choose attractive containers to hold functional items.

  » Be consistent so storage has a uniform look.

  » Label containers neatly so you know what's in them at a glance.

- Always be on the lookout for things you no longer want or need. Prune as you go to reduce clutter. Storing things that you won't really use (or need) costs precious time and energy, taking you away from relaxing. It's better to sell, donate, or dispose of these kinds of items.

- Choose finishes in kitchens, baths, and other "working rooms" that are low mainte-nance, durable, and visually appealing.

- Keep decorations simple in working rooms—a single bloom in a pretty vase or a single bowl of fruit is often enough to bring joy into a utilitarian space. Even cheerful but simple containers in pretty colors can stand in as "art and accessories" in hard-working and storage areas.

PART 3

EVERYDAY VACATION HOMES UP CLOSE

The following chapters highlight four unique homes in three disparate locations that follow the "vacation at home" philosophy while still expressing the unique personal styles and tastes of the homeowners. Our main house and adjacent carriage house at Rosemary Beach shown here are probably the most traditional of the four properties in terms of overall style. The main house is where Craig, Vera, Gavin, the pets, and I live when we are in Florida. We've also spent significant time living in the carriage house. It's now primarily where we put guests—and we know firsthand that we can accommodate a family of four comfortably in this small space! It lives large, as you'll see. Of course, neither of these houses is conventionally traditional, but I believe their design will feel familiar to most people, whereas the other two houses have a more contemporary and design-forward aesthetic.

All the homes manage to truly reflect the people living in them, yet all still use the same principles discussed in part 1. They replicate the calm, vacation-like feel for their homeowners, which means they start the process of relaxing, restoring, and reenergizing their inhabitants the minute they walk through the front door. Using the principles discussed throughout this book, each home has a focal point, which is either a spectacular view or a feature, they smell great, are quiet, and there's great texture in the homes. They also all employ symmetry to provide a sense of order and as a way of showcasing truly loved and meaningful items. Closed storage is used for functional but unsightly items. As a result, there is a place for all the odds and ends of bits and pieces of everyday life. There are so many other details that give these homes breathing room and a relaxing, restoring, and reenergizing vibe.

CHAPTER 6

BEACH RETREAT: ROSEMARY BEACH, FLORIDA

Let me just put it out there: no one would say our Rosemary Beach house is minimalist, even though it's soothing and spacious. It's a very warm home, and that is important to me. If someone is happy in a cooler, more austere environment, I say go for it. *This* house is tailored to us, so it is functionally supportive of our lives and stylistically reflective of the things that we love and that hold personal meaning for my family and for me.

Certain design decisions allude to being at the beach, but nothing is literal. I didn't want to decorate with mermaids and seahorses or a head-to-toe nautical look. There's nothing wrong with those design elements; they just aren't us. We wanted our second house in Rosemary Beach (we sold our first beach house, furniture and all, that was featured in my first book, *Design Wise!*) to be reflective of our journey as a family. For instance, in the summer of 2017, Craig and I took our kids, Gavin and Vera, to Europe for a month. It was a hard trip to pull off, not only because it was expensive but also because we both work for ourselves, and being away for that long can be a challenge. But it was so worth it. Traveling to diverse places is one of the most critical ways I stay inspired to design products and spaces.

This family adventure included trips to London, Paris, and areas of Sicily where we also happen to have dear friends. It was such a memorable experience, and we ended up bringing back objects we incorporated throughout the Rosemary Beach house to reflect our journey. We wanted to infuse the house with things that would remind us of being in those places and that were also whimsical and fun—after all, it *is* a beach house. For instance, we brought back a carousel animal from Paris (shown in our kitchen) and giant, white pottery pine cones from Sicily (it connotes enlightenment) that now sit in our courtyard.

In perhaps the strongest nod to the ocean, we had a good friend, Michael Boudreault of Artisan Rooms, paint a mural inspired by the famous painting *The Great Wave Off Kanagawa* by Hokusai, which we saw as a family in the British Museum in London. Per my request, Michael interpreted it in black, white, and various shades of gray, and it extends over three stories. I love it! It makes me happy to think of my friend Michael every time I look at it. In the foyer, I have a desk that is covered in a faux shagreen (or stingray skin) finish, which is also a nice nod to being at the beach without hitting you over the head. It has three drawers, which we use for car keys, dog leashes, mail, and other odds and ends of everyday life. I adorned several walls with multiple patterns of my own cleanable, easy-care wall covering. And every bedroom in the house that's outfitted with a television has a white box with the remote so no one has to look at a piece of black plastic. All these strategies work to make Rosemary Beach a place where we can focus on each other as a family.

CHAPTER 7

DESERT OASIS: ST. GEORGE, UTAH

This is the most minimalist of the homes you will see in this book and by far the one with the fewest accessories. It's reflective of the specific requests of the homeowners: calm, clean-lined, and more austere without being cold or uninhabitable. While it feels luxe, the design is rooted in principles that anyone can achieve. The monochromatic base or envelope of the interior (walls, floor, ceiling) is purposefully Zen in nature. These homeowners lead busy, stressful lives and needed this house to be an oasis of calm. For them, that meant pared down and light-filled with open areas and large-scale art but with a clear, unmistakable emphasis and focus on both the amazing views and comfortable living. Light, airy, and a blurring of the lines between outside and inside has been the design directive from day one.

There are moments in this house when you feel as if you are in a gallery. For instance, there is a windowless five-foot-wide hallway that runs through the house like a spine, and it is lined with nothing but over-scaled art. The result is unquestionably calming.

All the floors are honed limestone, which promotes a very warm feel, and having the same flooring material throughout provides a visual link while preventing the eye from distraction. It's soothing and reflective of their point of view.

Furniture and accessories were purposefully selected and placed with great intention to take in views, encourage social interaction, and enable relaxation.

The open, modern kitchen is outfitted with a large Macassar ebony island and dark brown Wenge perimeter cabinets that afford a bounty of storage. It flows easily into the living areas. Glass and windows make it bright and light. Perfect for cooking, entertaining, and most important relaxing.

This is a home designed to nurture its owners the minute they walk through the door.

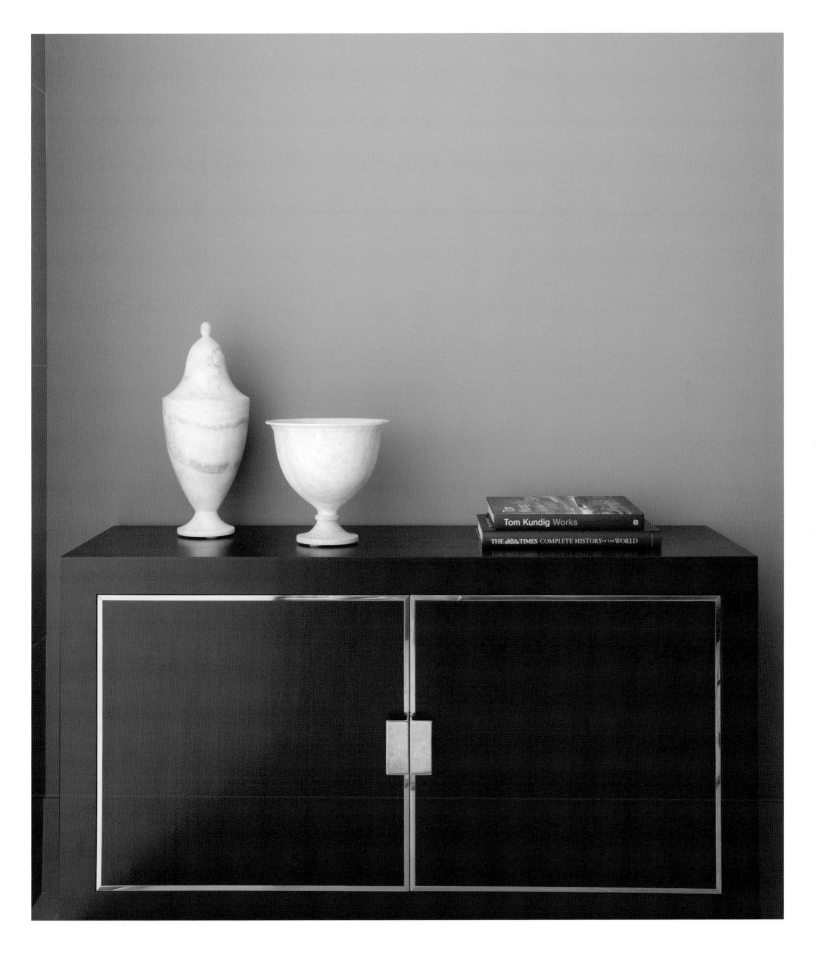

CHAPTER 8

WINTER WONDERLAND: PARK CITY, UTAH

This home is a contemporary take on a ski lodge, with an abundance of natural light and snowcapped mountain vistas. Anytime you have a location with dramatic views, you need to take advantage of them, and that was certainly my directive here. A variety of warm wall colors, including a plethora of warm grays that span mid-tones to nearly black in the master bedroom, are woven throughout and provide a welcoming counterpoint to the largely snow-covered exterior seen throughout a healthy portion of the year. Keeping the color palette consistent also allows the eye to relax as it seamlessly travels from space to space, allowing the focus to remain clearly on the views and a world-class art collection, which served as the main design jumping-off point in this home.

Of course, it is important that the eye knows where to go without unnecessary distraction. The homeowners' love of contemporary photography and painting is clearly reflected in their impressive and carefully curated collection. Putting what was meaningful and special to them on center stage was of utmost importance. They're also a fun, sporty, intellectual family of four (including two teenagers in college) who love to have a good time, so this home needed to reflect that as well. From a substantial media room with a Lord of the Rings pinball machine to plenty of dedicated space to accommodate a vast library of books, this home is indeed a unique and genuine real reflection of the family while still conveying calm and order.

CHAPTER 9

SMALL BUT RESTFUL: ROSEMARY BEACH, FLORIDA

Our Rosemary Beach carriage home comes in at a very efficient 590 square feet, complete with kitchen, laundry, and bathroom, yet it still houses up to four guests comfortably. It is essentially similar to a small one-bedroom apartment—or a hotel suite—and is likely not that different, square footage-wise, from the limited space that many people have to contend with every day. I used every strategy and technique in this book to pull off a tiny house that feels expansive and restful. Smart storage solutions in every possible corner maintain a sense of calm and relaxation. Careful space planning creates a sense of breathing room, restfulness, relaxation, and energizing visuals. No one feels they are missing anything in this space. No one feels cramped. It is intended for a family of four, after all!

It was important to me that no one felt this small space was hard to navigate. The sofa seats four people comfortably, and two swivel chairs accommodate more guests. Behind the sofa is a multipurpose console/kitchen island/dining table combination made out of low-maintenance Cambria quartz that matches the countertops on the adjacent kitchenette. It runs the length of the sofa and can serve as a prep area, dining table, and a desk. Its waterfall edges and smooth quartz material are visually elegant and simple. Mirrors on kitchen cabinet doors throw light around the room, making it even

brighter while concealing plenty of storage. There is even what I call a *foyer moment* in the house, so when you enter it, you feel the house is greeting you warmly, proving that even the smallest spaces can have a welcoming entryway. A consistent color palette of white walls, gray shagreen wall covering, and an accent color of citrine, a deep gold color, lets the eye comfortably travel from area to area seamlessly, thus increasing the perception of space.

Because of its location on the lot, it doesn't have the most sweeping of views—a feature (or lack thereof) that may be familiar to many people living in city apartments or small suburban houses. Instead of emphasizing a view through furniture placement, I had my muralist friend Michael Boudreault paint a scene on the largest wall that was inspired by a Hokusai exhibit our family saw in London. Instead of the iconic Hokusai piece that inspired the mural in the main Rosemary Beach house, we had Michael look at Hokusai images of mountains. Now, sparse clouds, a snowcapped mountain, a small house, and of course a dog—because we are a family of dog lovers—create an engaging visual that immediately directs your eye where to focus. It helps give the space a clear order much like a stunning view would. And like the large mural in the main house, it is done in shades of white, gray, and black so it has strength without overwhelming the interior.

APPENDICES

CHEAT SHEET:

THE IMPORTANT VACATION AT HOME PRINCIPLES

SMELL

It's important to be greeted by a clean, pleasant smell in your own home.

- Put shoes away as soon as you come home.
- Attend to dirty laundry as often as possible. Once it's a routine, it will become second nature.
- Use home fragrance devices (candles, diffusers, reeds, sprays, etc.). I have a collection of fragrance warmers, wax melts, diffusers, and candles that I designed with a resort feel in mind, but of course there are other great brands on the market, too. Find the ones you like!
- Take trash and recycling out of the house and into an outdoor receptacle as often as possible.

SOUND

Sound, or lack of it, can determine how you feel in your home. Many fine resorts make sure there is soft music playing in the background in all their public spaces (hallways, reception areas, elevators—but we've come a long way from elevator music!).

- If you don't have pleasing sounds of nature outside your door (or they are not accessible because of weather), consider creating a digital music playlist and invest in a Bluetooth speaker (for as little as twenty dollars) as part of an accessible system that makes playing your music easy as soon as you enter your home.
- If you're trying to muffle unwanted sound, use rugs, drapes, and plenty of other soft surfaces to help absorb those intrusive noises.

TOUCH

There are countless ways your body interacts with your home, and it's constantly taking cues from those interactions.

- Rugs underfoot are wonderful to step on when getting out of bed in the morning.
- Soft fabrics for upholstery make lounging even more pleasant—think velvet, chenille, easy-care linen blends, performance fabrics, and soft cottons. Indoor/outdoor fabrics, especially those manufactured with the new combination of solution-dyed polypropylene and high-energy polyester (look for the Inside Out Performance Fabrics label), can be practical for families with young children and animals because they offer softness alongside durability, stain resistance, fade resistance, and the ability to be cleaned with bleach.
- Fluffy towels are luxurious against the skin.
- Warm throws in cashmere, wool, or cotton keep you cozy on chilly nights.

SYMMETRY

Symmetry is one of the most powerful and useful tools in design.

- Chairs in pairs flanking a sofa are tidy and comfortable.
- Pairs of vases on a mantel are restful to the eye.
- Symmetrical cabinetry in the kitchen looks neat.
- Evergreen shrubbery (even in matching containers) on either side of your front door is stately and timeless.

FOCAL POINT

Every room should have a focal point.

- Views make natural focal points.
- A large piece of art can stand in for a missing view.
- A stately fireplace can ground a room and gather people in its glow.
- In windowless bathrooms, make a freestanding tub or a separate shower the main event.
- High headboards can be the major wow factor in any bedroom.
- A large vase of a single flower type can make a dining room.

BASIC MAINTENANCE

Recommended maintenance schedule:

- **Sheets:** Launder every four to five days with consecutive, daily use.
- **Bath towels:** Launder every three days with consecutive, daily use.
- **Hand towels:** Launder every two days with consecutive, daily use.
- **Vacuum:** Once a week for each person, dog, or cat in regularly and fully used areas. For example, a family of four with two dogs should vacuum six times a week in spaces inhabited by all. Master bedrooms used primarily by an individual or a couple may not necessitate vacuuming as frequently.

Recommended replacement schedule:

- **Bed pillow:** One to two years with regular, daily use.
- **Sheets:** Every two years with regular, daily use.
- **Down/feather comforter:** Fifteen to twenty years with annual professional cleaning.
- **Mattress:** Eight to ten years with regular, daily use.
- **Towels:** About every two years or when they lose their absorbency.

CHEAT SHEET:

THE EVERYDAY VACATION HOME BASICS

Here is my at-a-glance guide to the components that help create your vacation right at home:

1. **TELL THE STORY.** Set a relaxing and welcoming stage by presenting only the things you want to see—everything else that doesn't support your narrative should be put away.

2. **CREATE A GREAT FIRST IMPRESSION.** No matter how small your home may be, it's important to be warmly and calmly greeted when you first enter your home by a foyer or thoughtful entrance sequence.

3. **HAVE A FOCAL POINT.** Every room should have a clear focus, whether that's a view, fireplace, soaking tub, or large-scale piece of art.

4. **USE SYMMETRY.** This helps establish an order that we, as humans, are used to seeing. It's a natural part of our world and a great way to lend a sense of calm to a room.

5. **DESIGN FOR THE SENSES.** Smell, touch, and sound are just as important as sight.

6. **REFRESH THE VISUAL.** Change things up to keep it exciting like a hotel does. By switching things around occasionally, you'll better appreciate all your beloved items.

7. **RESET THE SPACE.** This includes making the bed, clearing the sink of dishes, and re-fluffing the sofa and throw pillows.

8. **SPACE PLAN.** Make sure to thoughtfully arrange your space to service you in the best way possible. If it feels full, pull an item or two out to create a bit of negative space.

9. **USE FEWER THINGS BUT BIGGER THINGS.** This will help minimize the visual clutter and help with strong and clear messaging in the room. This applies to artwork, furniture, mirrors, light fixtures, and so on.

10. **CONSIDER MONOCHROMATIC PALETTES.** Limiting the number of colors applied to the envelope of a space will help to relax the eye and mind.

11. **KEEP WHAT YOU LOVE AND WHAT YOU NEED.** Sell, donate, or dispose of the rest.

12. **TAKE ADVANTAGE OF CLOSED STORAGE.** Ensure that you have plenty of closed and purposeful storage to house life's necessities.

13. **ELEVATE WHAT YOU LOVE AND DISPLAY THOSE ITEMS PROPERLY.** Think like a museum and honor those items you choose to keep and want to be seen.

14. **SHOWCASE ORGANIC ITEMS.** It's nearly impossible to replace organic (like fruit or plants) items with replicas, so choose items that require less upkeep and offer the most bang for the buck.

15. **INSTALL DIMMERS WHERE POSSIBLE.** These should be on every switch and every lamp in your home.

16. **INCORPORATE THE COLOR WHITE.** It's powerful because it signifies cleanliness, which puts your mind at ease. It's why hotels only use white sheets and white towels.

17. **BUY QUALITY AND WHAT YOU LOVE.** It's important to purchase what you love and to purchase high-quality items that will last. Well-made items also often end up being less expensive in the long run because they're not replaced as often.

18. **SMARTLY MINIMIZE YOUR TO-DO LIST.** Select high-performance materials that will remove maintenance from your to-do list whenever possible.

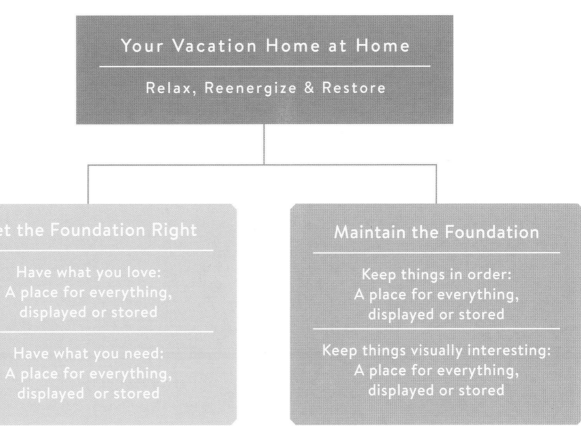

Your Vacation Home at Home

Relax, Reenergize & Restore

Get the Foundation Right

Have what you love:
A place for everything,
displayed or stored

Have what you need:
A place for everything,
displayed or stored

Maintain the Foundation

Keep things in order:
A place for everything,
displayed or stored

Keep things visually interesting:
A place for everything,
displayed or stored

RESOURCES

CABINETRY

Omega Cabinetry
812-482-2527
www.omegacabinetry.com

CARPETS & RUGS

Milliken Carpets
800-241-4826
www.milikenfloors.com

Myers Carpet and Flooring Center
Rugs, Carpeting, and Wood Flooring
866-450-5551
www.myerscarpet.com

DOOR & CABINET HARDWARE

Emtek Assa Abloy
800-356-2741
www.emtek.com

DOORS & WINDOWS

Marvin Windows and Doors
Windows and Exterior Doors
888-537-7828
www.marvin.com

TruStile
Interior Doors
877-283-4511
www.trustile.com

HOUSEHOLD EQUIPMENT

Bryant Heating and Cooling Systems
Air Conditioning and Heating
 Manufacturer
800-428-4326
www.bryant.com

Construction Resources
Appliances and Countertop Fabrication
404-378-3132
www.constructionresourcesusa.com

Ferguson
Bath and Kitchen Plumbing Fixtures and
 Sinks
800-638-8875
www.fergusonshowrooms.com

FABRIC & TRIM

Trend Fabrics
800-945-3838
www.trend-fabrics.com

FINE ART GALLERIES

Jackson Fine Art
404-233-3739
www.jacksonfineart.com

Sikkema Jenkins & Co.
212-929-2262
www.sikkemajenkinsco.com

FURNITURE & HOME DÉCOR

Anthropologie
800-309-2500
www.anthropologie.com

Aronson Woodworks
Handcrafted Solid Wood Furniture
515-707-2721
www.aronsonwoodworks.com

Bed Bath & Beyond
Bath and Kitchen Textiles and
 Accessories
800-462-3966
www.bedbathandbeyond.com

Boulevard, A Langley Empire Co.
Home Fragrance, Candles, and Décor
866-592-5514
www.langleyempirecandle.com
www.blvddecor.com

Charles P. Rogers
Beds, Mattresses, and Box Springs
800-582-6229
www.charlesprogers.com

The Container Store
Organization and Storage
888-266-8246
www.containerstore.com

Dedon
Outdoor Furniture
877-693-3366
www.dedon.us

Design Within Reach
800-944-2233
www.dwr.com

The Designer's Workroom
404-355-5080
www.thedesignersworkroomatlanta.com

duduc llc
Children's Furniture
212-226-1868
www.ducducnyc.com

Fabricut Furniture
833-662-7043
www.fabricut.com

Frette
Bedding and Towels
212-988-5221
www.frette.com

Mitchell Gold + Bob Williams
800-489-4195
www.mgbwhome.com

Oly Studio
844-354-2925
www.olystudio.com

RH, Restoration Hardware
800-762-1005
www.rh.com

Room & Board
800-301-9720
www.roomandboard.com

Saturday Knight Ltd.
Bath and Kitchen Textiles and
  Accessories
513-641-1400
www.saturdayknightlimited.com

West Elm
888-922-4119
www.westelm.com

William Sonoma Home
877-812-6235
www.wshome.com

LIGHTING

The Coppersmith Gas Lanterns
Gas Lanterns
800-249-1918
www.thecoppersmith.net

Ferguson Lighting Gallery
Decorative Lighting
800-638-8875
www.fergusonshowrooms.com

Stonegate by AFX
Decorative Lighting
847-249-5970
www.stonegatebyafx.com

USA Light and Electric
Recessed Lighting & Bulbs
877-235-0020
www.usalight.com

PAINT & WALL DÉCOR

Artisan Rooms
Custom Murals & Painting
614-940-4176
www.artisanrooms.com

Benjamin Moore Paint
855-724-6802
www.benjaminmoore.com

Sherwin-Williams Paint
800-474-3794
www.sherwin-williams.com

Trend Wallcovering
800-945-3838
www.trendfabrics.com

SOLID SURFACES

Cambria
Quartz Composite Surfaces, Natural
  Stone
866-226-2742
www.cambriausa.com

Emser Tile
Tile and Natural Stone
323-650-2000
www.emser.com

ACKNOWLEDGMENTS

Of the wide range of projects that I work on, from product designs for the home to room designs for television to architectural and interior designs for private clients, nothing has required more of my time and attention than the creation of my two books. It's an arduous process but one that I'm wholeheartedly enamored with because I know, firsthand, that books can be powerful instruments for change. I love that the good ones tend to stick around, get passed down, and become treasured and trusted companions. Behind each book is my hope that I've put something out into the world that will endure as a useful and invaluable tool to improve and transform people's lives by improving and transforming their homes. And to have any chance of accomplishing that, I've needed the backing, contributions, encouragement, support, and oftentimes understanding of so, so many. This second book would never have seen the light of day without the good folks mentioned below.

Thank you to my family. Everyone should be so lucky to be surrounded by a core circle so exceptionally loving and dedicated. Mom, Katherine, Bob, Rachel, George, Carl, Linda, Dave, Bonnie, Lucy, Sally, Uncle Joe, Aunt Annie, Carmen, Carter, Carson, Brooke, and Grayson: Your immense and unwavering encouragement and support lifts me up every day.

Thank you to my friends, an outstanding group of kind, thoughtful, smart, funny, loyal, and loving human beings. Mitch, Mia, Lauren D., Bob, Sara, James, Stacie, Paul, Holley, Alyssa, Dan K., Rob S., Deb, Thomas, Patrick, Matt, Gina, Barry, Jenya, David L., Rumaan, Anne Marie, Brant, Brian J., Ashley, Bill, Ryan L., Ross, Mila, Tyler J., Nassrin, Kevin, Brock, Holly, Arash, Rebecca, Derk, Darren, Lauren H., Elaine, Dan T., Leigh, Tom F., Rob M., Kim, MJ, Natalie, Tess, Michelle, John M., Britton, Olivia, Ryan W., Loren, David S., Sabrina, Margery, Steve, Caryl, Barron, Charles, Tyler A., Elisabeth, Leslie, Galen, Greg, Randy, John C., Angeli, Ajay, Amita, Tim, Jessica D. F., Michael B., Chris M., Chris W., Heather, Tyler M., Martha, Cynthia, Letsa, Clay, Megan, Clint, Kelly, Fianna, Daniel, Ginger, Jason V., Mary Alice, Wade, Millie, Sharon, Emily, Nina, Jennifer, Rebecca, Danica, Amber, David K., Dina, Jono, Jodi, Mat, AJ, Zoe, Jan, and David F.: My life is phenomenally better with you in it.

Thanks to the exceptional and talented professionals who helped make this book possible and who so expertly support me in my creative endeavors. Jeff Bernstein, Laura Nolan, David A. Land, Karen Kelly, Jennifer Kasius, Josh McDonnell, Kristin Kiser, Cisca Schreefel, Seta Zink, the team at Running Press, Claire Bamundo, David Finer, Millie Hammond, Sharon Cash, David Klaristenfeld, Bert Kerstetter, Bill Solomon, Tim Tevyaw, Bertha Hauser, George Jordan, Jim Lewis, Dianne Weidman, Kristin Vrsansky, Tonya Bott, Shanna Brichler, Jaimee Groves, Ron Hood, Laura De Pegna, Bruce Slavey, Dion Haynes, Summer Kath, Beth Garcia, Jamie Tanker, Aaron Komo, Gail Jameson, Matt Gustin, Michael Clinton, Sara Peterson, Meaghan Murphy, Jo Saltz, Sophie Donelson, Strand Conover, Meghan Mackenzie, Matthew Baskharoon, and the team at WME: your top tier talent, insight, and contributions have been invaluable and incredibly appreciated.

Special thanks to Rob and Deb Stone and Alise and Michael Khoury for allowing me to photograph their homes for inclusion in this book. It's been an honor and a privilege to design for you.

And thanks to our four-legged kids. Lars, Juno, Roo, and Wallace: I needed to rub your bellies almost more than you needed them rubbed.

Most of all, thanks to Craig, Gavin, and Vera. I'm so grateful to be going through life's journey with you. No matter what I accomplish, nothing will ever give me more happiness and pride than knowing that we are a family. You are, and will always be, the first faces I want to see in the morning and the last faces I want to see before I go to bed.

For helping to make it possible for me to practice interior design for over twenty-five years, work in television for nearly twenty years, design over a thousand home products, and create this second book, I also want to express my immense gratitude to the fans who've helped open all of these wonderful doors and more. May your home always feel like the most special and nurturing place on the planet. I'm humbled by, and grateful for, your support.

ENDNOTES

1. "Steve Jobs' 2005 Stanford Commencement Address: 'Your Time Is Limited, So Don't Waste It Living Someone Else's Life,'" *Huffington Post*, October 5, 2011, www.huffingtonpost.com/2011/10/05/steve-jobs-stanford-commencement-address_n_997301.html.

2. acoba Urist, "When the Gospel if Minimalism Collides with Daily Life," *New York Times*, April 29, 2017, www.nytimes.com/2017/04/29/style/when-the-gospel-of-minimalism-collides-with-daily-life.html.

3. "What Is an Appliance Garage?," Kitchen Cabinet Kings, www.kitchencabinetkings.com/glossary/appliance-garage/.

4. "USDA Plant Hardiness Zone Map," US Department of Agriculture, www.planthardiness.ars.usda.gov/PHZMWeb/.

INDEX